MW01289798

Math Gold

How to improve your high school math score dramatically

in 3 or 4 weeks, without a private tutor.

Al Pasha

www.mathgold.net

This book is dedicated to the loving

memory of my mother, Zeenath.

Higher Score Guaranteed or your money back.
General conditions apply.

*This book is available on Amazon. Download the free Kindle App.
Click on any topic in the Table of Contents to reach it instantly.*

Table of Contents

Foreword

Based on eleven years of actual teaching experience with the Sacred Heart Academy and Kaplan, Inc., plus eight years as an independent private math tutor, the author provides valuable and practical advice on how you can quickly and easily improve your math SAT or ACT scores in the shortest possible time.

Practical tips on strategy and tactics are provided along with guidance on which topics appear more frequently in the SAT and ACT tests, what you need to know, and what you may safely omit.

The SAT and ACT Tests are life-changing events. They decide which college or university you will go to and what your future career and life may look like.

Given automation and artificial intelligence, the world is becoming more competitive, and jobs will be even more difficult to find without a good college degree.

This book will immediately help students who cannot afford the high cost of a private tutor. It is written to be easily understood by the average teenager on their own.

This small book discusses some 92 different math topics.

Preface

Nearly one-half of the SAT Test is math. Whether or not you believe it now, math impacts all aspects of your life and career. Your level of expertise in high school math and your test score can determine how easily and well you will sail through college. Knowledge of math will also help you in the study of most subjects and make them that much easier for you.

My purpose in writing this book is first to review and advance your knowledge of high school math. Secondly, to help you directly maximize your SAT or ACT math test scores based on what you have learned. It takes four to five years to study math in high school, and there are excellent textbooks available to teach you math. However, there are fewer comprehensive books available on techniques, strategies, and tactics to maximize your standardized test scores.

Many books on the SAT/ACT tests are available in the marketplace from reputable publishers (such as Kaplan, McGraw-Hill, Barron's, Princeton, Khan Academy, etc.). Each of these books covers both Math and English and can often be 1000 pages long. In math, their focus is on test problems, providing answers with detailed explanations.

This relatively small book complements these works and focuses on what a private tutor would tell you (as I do) when working with you individually. It explains key math concepts, the structure of the tests, what occurs frequently, and what is less essential. It discusses strategy and tactics for the tests and gives you many practical tips on solving problems quickly and easily and on time management during the tests. Currently, not many books exist in the marketplace which focus on what it takes to improve your score substantially in the least amount of time.

The thinking behind this book is that you should learn these unique strategies and tactics in as short a period of time as possible and improve your math test score by some 70-90 points in SAT (or 6 to 8 points in ACT) or more in maybe 3 to 4 weeks of dedicated study of this book. The specialized knowledge contained in this book, based on vast experience, is like gold to students taking the SAT and ACT math tests and for high school math in general.

This book is not light reading, and you are studying with important life goals in mind. So have a target score in mind; grab a yellow marker and a red pen and settle down to study intensely for the next few days. Some of it will not be easy, but you will undoubtedly emerge many times stronger than when you started!

I have kept the cost of this book as low as possible to allow the maximum number of students to benefit. A modern textbook on math or precalculus these days can cost twenty times as much!

The second edition of this book, MATH GOLD tpe, describes how teachers and parents can also help their students and kids improve their math scores in school and on the SAT/ACT texts.

Private Tutoring

I was an elite tutor with the largest Learning Center in the USA for exactly ten years and have since been entirely independent in the last eight years. During these periods, and earlier, I have tutored more than 700 students either in a classroom or on a one-to-one basis and have produced excellent results, both in terms of scores and scholarships achieved.

While so far, some 18 of my students have achieved perfect scores of 800 in SAT or 36 in ACT, many more have come close and achieved excellent results, leading at times to scholarships.

I also pay particular attention to helping below-average students. Based on final results, parents have often provided me with excellent testimonials, as can be seen on my website www.calculus-math-tutor.com

During the course of my long career in teaching, I realized that not all students have equal access to good tutoring in school math or for the SAT and ACT. Private tutoring can often be expensive, and many parents do not have adequate financial resources. This fact alone, and my desire to help students directly, has motivated me to write this book.

My thinking is to help level the playing field for all students. In writing this book, I hope to help thousands of students, instead of just a few hundred directly, who may otherwise not have access to my specialized knowledge and years of experience of teaching the standardized tests.

Almost all of what I have written in MATH GOLD and MATH GOLD tpe is based on my own professional expertise and experience. The views and opinions expressed here are mine alone and not of any other party.

Leading Learning Centers

Learning centers are where many students go for tutoring services to improve their scores on various standardized tests such as the SAT, ACT, PSAT, SSAT, ISEE, and Regents. These are often large companies that market their services on a nationwide basis and who are not hesitant to charge high fees. I was myself an elite tutor with the largest of these organizations.

While these learning centers do teach some high school math, they mostly market their tutorial services to parents by suggesting that they teach strategies and tactics to help their kids improve their test scores quickly and easily. These are mostly tricks or shortcuts to answer questions, which may or may not work in all circumstances.

I explain some of these popular strategies below:

Deleting answer choices: It is a natural tendency with students who do not know how to correctly solve a problem, to look at answers, and start deleting choices which they think do not make sense. This is little more than just guesswork.

Picking numbers: Here, the idea is to pick any number, usually small, and plug it into the problem to produce an answer; then, plug the same number into each of the multiple-choice answers and see which matches. This is your answer. If two answers match, you will have to pick another number and rework the problem to isolate one response. This process may take time.

Many of these tricks do produce the correct multiple-choice answer to a question, but not always. Plugging in a number such as 2 or 3 may work, but using 1 or 0 can provide varying, unreliable answers. Also, there is no guarantee that working with negative or fractional numbers (like one-half) would produce the same response.

I am not a great believer in tricks and shortcuts and would rather teach students the basic math necessary to solve problems quickly and accurately in all circumstances.

Backsolving is a valid strategy and works well in some situations, where it provides valid answers and may even save some time. The most common situation is with so-called word problems that describe real-life situations. Here, you choose one of the four or five multiple choices provided and see if it works. You feed the number in that choice into the problem and if it works, that is your answer. If not, you choose another answer and repeat it.

The main problem with backsolving is that we cannot apply it in most circumstances, but when it works, it does well.

In the old SAT test there was negative marking, and you had a quarter-point deducted if your answer was wrong. Guessing, therefore, didn't always make sense then. Now, with no negative marking in the test, you should always guess when you do not know how to solve a problem. First, see if you can eliminate any answers logically and then guess from the remaining choices. If you have no clue at all, guess randomly from the choices.

Tricks and strategies may sound exciting to some students and their parents, but they are not always effective. Also, they may take longer than it would to solve the problem logically.

Therefore, my suggestion to the student would be to focus on learning basic math first, particularly algebra 1 and 2, and then think about tricks and shortcuts. You will be better off that way.

One rarely sees substantial increases in test scores at learning centers. This may be because of their focus on tricks and shortcuts, instead of adequately teaching basic math. Also, many math tutors are part-timers, inexperienced, or not formally trained in teaching.

Large hikes in scores are only possible with a student's own dedicated efforts, with or without a private tutor. Interested parents are always helpful and the strongest motivating force for a student.

SAT vs. ACT Math Tests

Some students, and their parents, have difficulty choosing between taking the SAT and the ACT tests. This choice obviously depends on many factors, but in this section, I shall focus only on the math portion of the tests.

The ACT originated on the West Coast and has now gained more popularity in the East. The math part of the ACT is somewhat easier than the new version of the SAT. However, it is accompanied by the Science Test, which is not on the SAT. While no prior knowledge of science is required, the science test itself poses a significant challenge to some students – many take it in their stride while others have difficulty.

The science test on the ACT currently contains seven passages, all based on scientific information from biology, physics, chemistry, astronomy, etc. Again, no prior knowledge of science is necessary, and enough relevant scientific information is provided in the passage itself. The student is given 5 minutes per passage with 4 or 5 questions in each, for a total of 35 minutes for the science test.

The ACT math test has 60 problems and allows for one hour. The SAT math test is in two parts with 20 and 38 problems, allowing 25 minutes and 55 minutes, respectively, for a total time of 80 minutes. The smaller section of the SAT does not permit the use of a calculator. Both parts have questions with multiple-choice answers and some quantitative answers. Scores reach a maximum of 36 on the ACT and 800 on the SAT, and there is no pass or fail.

Common mathematical formulas (such as $A = \pi r^2$) are provided on the SAT at the beginning of each section. The ACT, however, does not provide formulas to the test taker (except for rare situations within a problem, such as for the volume of a sphere, law of cosines, etc.)

The new SAT math test is now more difficult than in the past and includes some trigonometry and precalculus. There are fewer geometry questions, but the level of knowledge required to solve those remaining has not been lowered.

Time is always an issue in the tests   even more so with the ACT than with the SAT. The ACT allows an average of 1 minute per problem. With the SAT the average time is under one and a half minutes. In my experience, more students tend to drop problems in the ACT toward the end of the test.

Also, since the SAT math test is in two sections, it allows the student to recover if he or she messes up the timing in the first section.

To conclude, given that both tests have their benefits and drawbacks, you   should look at and try out both math tests before finally deciding which one to focus on, or take both!

What's in the Math tests?

No need to memorize formulas

Previously all SAT math was essentially 10th-grade math, consisting of Arithmetic, Algebra, and Geometry, with some Precalculus, and hardly any Trigonometry. With the new SAT, introduced in 2016, there is much more precalculus and trigonometry, with reduced emphasis on geometry problems. I cover most of the additional math in this book.

Algebra

Of the five main topics above in math, algebra is by far the most important. If you are not good at it, you are unlikely to score well in other parts of math. Algebra 1 & 2 is essentially a set of rules and procedures which describe how to model and deal with real-life situations. For example, P-E-M-D-A-S says that in dealing with an expression or equation, you should start with parenthesis first, then exponents, followed by multiplication, division, addition and, finally, subtraction, strictly in that order. Violate this rule even once and your answer will immediately be wrong!

Algebra is mostly taught in school from Grade 7 onwards and is built on gradually over three to four years. We will deal with many of the situations that arise in the tests, but let me emphasize that constant practice is essential. The <u>negative</u> sign in algebra or math is very important and may appear two or three times simultaneously in a problem. Ignore any one of these negatives and you will be wrong.

Here's a common situation which students often handle incorrectly: Given -(a+b), some students will distribute, or remove the brackets, by writing the expression as –a+b, whereas it should be –a-b. This might seem obvious to you right now, but in the midst of a lot of algebraic activity, it is easy to go wrong. One simple mistake like this and a lot of prior good work is lost!

Plane Geometry

Students sometimes ask me: Why do we have to learn geometry? Why do we need it? To this, I answer that, first and foremost, it teaches you the deductive, or logical, process. It is the system of analysis that Sherlock Holmes, the famous detective, used whereby he established all the facts first and then, by strictly logical reasoning, reached valid conclusions. You should use the same approach in solving geometry problems.

Typically, you are provided charts or diagrams in standard geometry problems. If not, you should immediately sketch something to begin with and clearly note the facts given in the problem. Then, based on the rules, syllogisms, or theorems you have learned in geometry, you should draw conclusions one by one, leading to the final answer you require. This deductive process requires that you take one step at a time and not jump to conclusions.

The number of geometry problems in the new SAT test has been reduced, but the level of knowledge required remains the same. There is a lot to be learned in geometry, but most of it is fairly straightforward if you start slowly and work gradually. I list the main topics for you below. Trigonometry takes over where geometry leaves off and was not on the SAT before 2016.

You should know the following topics in geometry:

Lines and angles.

Triangles: perimeter, area, similarity, congruence, etc.

Quadrilaterals and Polygons: internal angles, perimeters and areas.

Parallel lines and transversals: vertically opposite angles, corresponding angles; alternate interior angles, same side interior angles, etc.

Perimeters and areas of rectangles, parallelograms, rhombuses, trapezoids, and polygons.

Circles: radius, diameter, area and circumference, sectors, chords, secants, and tangents.

Conics: parabolas, ellipses, hyperbolas, etc.

Solid figures are discussed separately below.

Coordinate & Solid Geometry

With coordinate geometry, it is even more important to sketch a diagram or chart for each problem. This type of geometry arises when you are given the coordinates (x, y). If you do not sketch the problem, it is easy to go wrong.

Every graph has four quadrants (I, II, III and IV). If either x, y or both are negative the quadrant will change dramatically, and you will get incorrect answers. Many students try to visualize the situation in their head without sketching a diagram and often go wrong. I emphasize this repeatedly to students.

Plane geometry is in two dimensions, on a single plane, with two x and y axes. With three dimensions, you have to add a third dimension, z-axis, vertical to the first two axes.

Solid geometry, in three dimensions, consists of solid figures such as rectangular solids, prisms, cylinders, cones, pyramids, and others.

You might think that there is a whole range of formulas to memorize to calculate volumes and surface areas of these solids. In my view, this is not necessary, if you understand a few basics about these bodies.

Most solid figures that appear on the SAT or ACT have bases with vertical heights and the volume of the solid is the area of the rectangular or circular base multiplied by the vertical height. In other words, Volume = length x width x height = area of base x height. Simple!

For a cylinder, the principle is the same, and Volume = area of base x height. This time the base is circular, which means $A = \pi r^2$. This multiplied by the height of the cylinder is the volume. $V = \pi r^2 h$, where h is the height.

For point-top figures such as cones and pyramids, the volume is simply one-third of the volume of the corresponding cylinder or rectangular solid, or $\frac{1}{3}\pi r^2 h$ or $\frac{1}{3}lwh$ respectively. Don't ask me why the fraction is one-third!

The total **surface area** of a rectangular solid is the sum of the areas of six two-dimensional surfaces and is given by $S = 2(lw + lh + wh)$, where l, w and h represent length, width and height respectively.

The total surface area of a pyramid is the sum of the areas of the base and four triangles. The entire surface area of a cone is slightly more complicated and is given by the sum of the area of the base $A=\pi r^2$ and the lateral surface, $S=\pi rl$, where r is the radius of the circular base and l is the slant height. (The slant height is the hypotenuse of a right-angled triangle, with the vertical height as one leg and the radius as the second leg.)

Usually, no more than one or two problems on solid geometry appear on the standardized tests. There are many more such problems in the Math Subject Tests, Levels 1 & 2.

Note: A key feature of many rectangular solid geometry problems appearing in the regular SAT and ACT is that they involve using the Pythagorean Theorem twice, once vertically and another time horizontally. The horizontal right angle triangle lies in the base of the solid figure. The vertical right triangle is perpendicular to the first triangle and usually involves the diagonal passing through the solid figure. If you remember this, and are able to identify the two right-angled triangles, you will be able to deal with this type of problem readily.

(To visualize this better, you may have to refer to a text-book with drawings of rectangular solid figures.)

Arithmetic

We cannot forget arithmetic! It is the basic building block for all math but often ignored as being too easy. In reality, some of the arithmetic problems in SAT or ACT, when they occur, involve counting and can be hard. The new SAT places emphasis on arithmetic, since it disallows the use of a calculator in one of the two math sections.

Far too often, I see students using their calculators when it is a matter of simple mental arithmetic. For example, 9 times 8 should not require a calculator. Get into the habit now of not using the calculator when possible and you will see a rapid drop in the time needed to complete problems, with fewer errors.

Some of the more difficult problems in the math tests involve simple arithmetic and counting only. These may start with data analysis problems, rising to Venn diagrams, permutations, simple probability, and the like.

When using a calculator, be sure to type negatives, parenthesis, fractions, exponents, etc. carefully so as to avoid mistakes. With negative numbers and fractions, and the use of brackets, it is easy to make mistakes while punching numbers into the calculator.

What is a prime number? A prime number only has 1 and itself as factors. For example, 13 is prime because it has only 1 and 13 as factors.

In the two standardized tests, please remember that 1 is not a prime number. Also, that 2 is prime as well as an even number. Again, zero is an even number just because the following number is odd. Many students either do not realize all this or do not remember.

Scientific Notation simply says that there should be only one digit before the decimal point, multiplied by a power of 10. For example, 7,632,874 should be written as 7.632874×10^6; and 0.0035682 should be written as 3.5682×10^{-3}. That's all there is to it!

Precalculus

The old SAT test did not have much precalculus. It does now, with a significant amount of trigonometry. In some ways, precalculus is more difficult than calculus itself, since it contains several different concepts, whereas calculus generally is confined to three main concepts: limits, differentiation and integration. Most of the relevant topics in precalculus and trigonometry are discussed in this book and those omitted do not appear all that often in the SAT or ACT tests.

To do well in precalculus and, later in calculus, your foundation in algebra 2 should be strong. Therefore, if you are weak in algebra, I would advise that you go back and relearn the rules and techniques of algebra, and practice because you will need to know them fluently.

Trigonometry 1

Trigonometry is not a difficult subject and most students pick it up quickly. However, I have seen some schools or teachers complicate the subject matter unnecessarily.

You should know that a Unit Circle means a circle with a radius of one. I haven't found this concept particularly useful, but some textbooks make a big deal out of it.

Know also that an angle on a coordinate plane is measured counter-clockwise and that the negative angle is measured clockwise.

You should know how to measure angles in degrees and radians. A radian is defined by the angle formed at the center of a circle by an arc (on the circumference) exactly equal in length to the radius of the circle. It is equal to approximately 57.3 degrees.

The circumference of a circle is given by $2\pi r$, so if we divide the circumference into arcs of length r, we will have 2π equal arcs, and each arc will measure one radian at the center of the circle. Since the angle at the center of a circle is 360 degrees, 2π radians is equal to 360°. If you can remember this, you can always figure that one radian is equal to $\frac{360}{2\pi}$ degrees, or $\frac{180}{\pi}$ degrees.

Within a right-angled triangle, Sine is defined as the Opposite side divided by the Hypotenuse, Cosine=Adjacent side/Hypotenuse and Tangent=Opposite side/Adjacent side. All of this is summarized succinctly in "SOHCAHTOA". The remaining three trigonometric functions cosec, sec and cot are the reciprocals of sine, cos and tan respectively. This means that $\csc x = \frac{1}{\sin x}$, etc.

The coordinate plane divides into four quadrants: I, II, III and IV. All trigonometric ratios are positive in the first quadrant; only sine is positive in the second quadrant; tan is positive in the third and cos in the fourth quadrant. This is summarized by A-S-T-C, or "All Students Take Calculus!" The quadrant determines the sign of the trigonometric function.

In order to calculate angles in the other three quadrants II, III and IV, you need to determine the 'reference angle' first by visualizing a Bow Tie with its intersection at the origin (0, 0). Any reference angle calculated must lie within the bow tie.

Once the reference angle is known, you can determine the trigonometric ratios from the first quadrant and determine the sign (+ or -) according to the A-S-T-C rule. For example, the reference angle of 210° is 30° in the third quadrant (since 30° is within the bow tie). So, if you are looking for sine 210°, it is the same as the sine of 30° (which is ½), and since sine is negative in the third quadrant according to ASTC, the answer is -1/2.

Most of the common trigonometric ratios can be calculated by using special triangles 30°-60°-90° or 90°-45°-45°. You should know the ratio of the three sides of a special triangle, although this is given to you on the SAT Test.

For a 30°-60°-90° triangle the ratio is $1:\sqrt{3}:2$. And, for example,

sine 60° is equal to $\frac{\sqrt{3}}{2}$. (Remember that the side opposite 60° is greater than for 30°, and $\sqrt{3}$ is greater than 1.)

For a 90°-45°-45° triangle the ratio is $\sqrt{2}:1:1$, and both sine 45° and cos 45° are equal to $\frac{1}{\sqrt{2}}$.

It is not necessary to memorize common trigonometric values if you know how to set up the two special triangles with the correct ratios.

Know the five special angles above and you will be able to determine many other angles (e.g., 15° and 75°) using trigonometric formulas and identities described later.

Trigonometry, initially is a study of triangles: A triangle has 3 sides and 3 angles, making a total of 6 elements. Given any 3 components, the student should be able, using trigonometry, to determine the 3 remaining elements.

Note: The previous section assumed some prior knowledge of trigonometry, and is a summary of the main concepts for the tests. If this section was difficult to follow, please refer to a basic textbook on trigonometry and refresh your knowledge. Also, there is more in the section on Trigonometry 2 below.

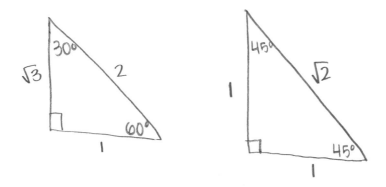

Two Important Topics in the Tests

Algebra goes a long way

Three algebraic identities

Normally, I do not ask my students to memorize formulas. This is because within 2 to 3 weeks of the tests, they are likely to forget the formulas. Even if they do recall them, they may not be sure that they remember correctly.

However, there are three algebraic identities which I insist that they remember for both the SAT and ACT. These should be inscribed in the brain in such a manner that even if someone wakes them up in the middle of the night in their sleep and asks them, they should be able to recite them! That's how important these identities are. They appear all the time on both tests in various shapes and forms. They are simple but vital to the tests.

Identities occur when the two sides of an equation are always equal for all values of the variables. For example, ab-bc+3 = 3+b(a-c) is a simple identity.

Know always the square of a+b. That is, what is $(a+b)^2$ equal to? It may seem simple, but many students say a^2+b^2 and forget the middle term 2ab. Please always remember that

$(a+b)^2 = a^2+2ab+b^2$. This is the first identity.

Similarly, $(a-b)^2 = a^2-2ab+b^2$, which is the second identity. Remember that the middle term is negative.

A third identity occurs even more often than the first two in math tests. It is the difference of two squares, that is, a^2-b^2. Please remember that whenever you see this expression, it can be factored into (a+b) (a-b), so that:

a^2-b^2=(a+b) (a-b). If you FOIL the right-hand side, you can verify the identity.

This third identity often appears in a disguised form in some problems in both tests. For example, if you see x^2-9, immediately break it down to (x+3) (x-3). It is that simple. Do not try anything fancy or sophisticated, such as using the quadratic formula, although the expression is technically a quadratic. If you do, you will not get anywhere and may not be able to solve the problem, and you will waste a lot of time.

Special Triangles

Special triangles are unbelievably important; although this time, and unlike the algebraic identities above, they are given to you at the beginning of each SAT Test. I also use them extensively in teaching trigonometry, and this avoids having to memorize several formulas.

Special triangles use the Pythagorean Theorem, and there are two important cases to remember. Recall that Pythagoras applies only to right-angled triangles, and the two situations are $90°$-$45°$-$45°$ and $30°$-$60°$-$90°$ triangles.

The $90°$-$45°$-$45°$ triangle is isosceles, and the ratios of the three sides is 1:1:$\sqrt{2}$.

For the $30°$-$60°$-$90°$ triangle, the ratios are 1:$\sqrt{3}$:2. Know that 2 is the longest side, and is therefore the hypotenuse. The side facing the $60°$ angle is $\sqrt{3}$ and bigger than the side facing the $30°$ angle.

Memorize the ratio of the three sides of these two special triangles and it will help you enormously in geometry (plane, coordinate, and solid) and trigonometry.

[Note that I have dropped the 's' shown in the formulas provided in the SAT tests since I have stated them as ratios, whereas they write them as lengths of sides. Also, when in doubt, simply use the Pythagorean Theorem to verify that you remember the ratios correctly.]

A third special triangle is the 3-4-5 special right-angle triangle. Note that $3^2+4^2=5^2$ is Pythagoras. All multiples of 3-4-5 (such as 6-8-10, 9-12-15, etc.) also work and knowing this will save you time on the standardized tests.

Again, 5-12-13 and 8-15-17 work as right-angled triangles and are worth remembering.

Some Practical Tips for the Two Tests

Simplify, simplify, and simplify

Must read carefully

It is important to read problems very carefully – just one word can change the answer. Words like integer, positive or negative, odd or even, inclusive, additional, another, etc. are critical.

In many cases, you will have to read a problem more than once to clearly understand what is being said. This is par for the course.

Always simple solutions

Generally speaking, and in my opinion, the answers to all problems in the two standardized tests are nearly always simple. Only a few of the problems require more than 3 or 4 lines to answers. Rarely, will you see the answer go to 6 or 7 lines. If that happens, there is something wrong and you have probably misunderstood the question. Examiners do realize that you have limited time available, so they do not give burdensome problems in the test.

Always simplify at every opportunity

A cardinal rule in high school math is always to simplify first. For example, if you can simplify both sides of an equation by dividing by, say 2 do so first, before you move on. You will be amazed at the difference it makes in arithmetic and algebra, particularly in situations such as factoring and solving equations, etc.

If you are given a fraction like $\dfrac{14}{16}$, you will automatically simplify it to $\dfrac{7}{8}$. Doing this in arithmetic problems is almost a reflex action, so why not in algebra?

If you have a number or variable in the numerator of a fraction and the same number or variable appears in the denominator, cancel both and make your life easier. For example, given $\dfrac{3ab^2}{6bz}$, you should promptly simplify it to $\dfrac{ab}{2z}$.

When an addition or subtraction is involved in the numerator or denominator, you cannot simplify as in the last paragraph. This is a strict no-no! For example, $\dfrac{a+b}{b-c}$ cannot be simplified by canceling out the b's.

Sometimes, if you do not simplify an algebraic expression when possible, you may not see what the next step could be and may not know how to proceed. The simple act of getting rid of extraneous numbers and variables makes progress smoother.

Finally, remember that the multiple-choice answers in the standardized tests are nearly always in their most simplified form. Fractions should be reduced to their lowest form, and decimal answers should normally have three significant digits. For example, 3.47 and 0.875 each have three significant digits. The latter should preferably be written as a fraction $\dfrac{7}{8}$ on the computer answer sheet.

Answer what is required

The rule is to always focus on what the question is asking you for, not what you think it is asking for. For example, if the problem asks for the value of (x+y), prefer to go looking for the value of x and y together and not separately. Don't always think that you will find x first and then y and then add them together. Sometimes, especially in geometry, you may not be able to find x and y separately, whereas you will be able to determine (x+y). Often, in this type of situation, it is easier to find the combined value of (x+y).

I repeat, always focus directly on what any problem is asking from you.

Increasing order of difficulty

You should know that test problems are progressive in terms of difficulty, certainly on the SAT, with the easier problems occurring in the beginning and the more difficult ones appearing later. With the

ACT there is no such clear progression but, to date, the last 10 problems out of the total 60 are usually distinctly harder.

As a tutor, I always pay attention to where I am in a section of 20 or 38 problems in the SAT. This tells me immediately how easy or difficult a problem is likely to be, even before I have read it. If a student gives me a complicated answer to an early problem, I ask him to rethink it. Similarly, if he or she comes up with a simple answer for a near-end problem, I again ask the student to reread and rethink the problem.

I suggest that you always recognize where you are in the SAT test: beginning, middle or towards the end. This will help you anticipate the level of difficulty of the problem you are dealing with. If you come up with a complicated answer to an early problem, you are likely to have misunderstood the question. Likewise, if you come up with a very simple answer to a late problem, think again! Of course, there are always going to be exceptions, but I haven't really seen that many variations.

The last four problems in a test or section are usually the hardest. By the time you reach there, you may be running out of time. There is no law saying that you have to answer them in the order in which they are presented to you. Glance at all four problems and see which ones look easier and answer those first. If a question looks difficult, or you don't like it, just guess the answer and move on!

Additional difficult problems

There are other specific problems in a math test which are known to be difficult:

The two math sections in the SAT Test are divided into two parts each – multiple choice and quantitative (or grid-in) answers. Problems towards the end of each of these two sub-sections tend to be harder than the others. Therefore, watch out for problems 13, 14 and 15 in Section 3 of the SAT Test and 35 to 38 in Section 4.

With the ACT the structural layout of the problems is a lot simpler. The first 50 out of the total 60 questions are broadly similar in level of difficulty. The last ten or so problems are distinctly harder! When I work with stronger students, I usually focus on the last ten problems only. This way, their skill and confidence level are built up rapidly and they perform better on the tests.

Always remember <u>not</u> to spend too much time on difficult problems. They carry the same marks as the easier problems. First, solve the easier problems and then go for the harder ones. It is important to try to complete the test because dropping problems toward the end of a test is like getting them wrong. If you prefer, mark the harder problems without spending any time on them and come back to them later if you have time. If you cannot come back, you have only dropped problems that were hard for you in the first place!

As a rule, watch out for difficult problems and, if you can't deal with them, guess them anyway! There is no negative marking now in both the SAT and ACT tests, which means that a student is not penalized for getting an answer wrong. I deal with this topic extensively in another section on time management later in this book.

Essential High School Math

The Pythagorean Theorem (or simply Pythagoras) is the most famous formula in high school math: $\mathbf{a^2 + b^2 = c^2}$, where a and b are the sides of a right-angled triangle and c is the hypotenuse.

Most high school students are aware of this formula, but some forget that it applies to right-angled triangles only. For other types of triangles, you need geometry and trigonometry.

Linear Equations

Everyone should know what $y = mx+b$ represents. It is a linear equation or the equation of a straight line. The 'm' stands for the slope of the line and could be positive or negative. (If m=0, there is no slope, and the equation represents a horizontal line). The 'b' is the y-intercept, or where the line cuts the y-axis, and again can be positive or negative. A zero y-intercept makes the line go through the origin. The equation would then be $y = mx$

The slope of a line, m, is the rise divided by the run (or $\frac{rise}{run}$) and is given by the rise ($y_2 - y_1$) divided by the run ($x_2 - x_1$). This is the gradient of the line and tells you how fast or slowly the line rises or falls. Slope $= \frac{(y2 - y1)}{(x2 - x1)}$.

If you are given an equation in x and y, you have to convert it first to the standard form above in order to sketch a graph of the line. Take for example 2y=3x-7. Dividing both sides by 2 converts the equation to the standard form $y = \frac{3}{2}x - \frac{7}{2}$. You can see that the slope of the line is a positive $\frac{3}{2}$ and the y-intercept is negative at $-\frac{7}{2}$. It is now easy enough to sketch the line. A positive slope goes up to the right, whereas a negative figure slopes backward to the left.

If the equation had been 2x=7-3y, it would produce a very different standard form $y = -\frac{2}{3}x + \frac{7}{3}$. This line would cut the y-axis at

$+\frac{7}{3}$ and have a slope going up to the left with a rise of 2 for a run of 3. You can check this yourself.

The point at which the line cuts the x-axis is the solution to the linear equation. This is because at this point, the value of y is zero. In the first example above, if you plug in y=0, the equation becomes 3x-7=0, so that the x-intercept, or the solution to the equation, is $x=\frac{7}{3}$. In the second equation above, the solution is $x=\frac{7}{2}$.

Questions about straight lines, slopes, intercepts and solutions to equations occur all the time on the SAT and ACT tests. The student need not memorize anything if he or she understands what is happening.

Midpoint of a Straight Line

How do you find the midpoint of a straight line? The average of the two end x-coordinates gives you the mid x-coordinate. Similarly, the average of the two end y-coordinates gives you the mid-y coordinate. You need not memorize the mid-point formula if you understand this.

Point of Intersection

Two different linear equations in x and y will represent two straight lines. The two lines (if not parallel) will intersect at one point somewhere. The x and y-coordinates of this intersection point give you the values of x and y that solve the two equations. You can either read these two coordinates on a graph or solve the two equations simultaneously, as you would normally by substitution or elimination.

Distance Formula

You do not have to memorize the distance formula either if you know that it is derived simply from the Pythagorean formula. All you have to do is construct a right-angled triangle based on the two points and their x- and y-coordinates.

Let's assume the two points are given by the coordinates (x_1, y_1) and (x_2, y_2). Connecting the points with a straight line would give you the distance between the two points, which we shall call 'd'. Make this the hypotenuse of a right-angled triangle and apply Pythagoras, as follows:

Pythagoras is $a^2+b^2 = c^2$, where a and b are the legs of a right-angled triangle, and c is the hypotenuse. The difference between the x-coordinates or (x_2-x_1) is one leg of the right-angled triangle and the difference between the y-coordinates (y_2-y_1) is the other leg. Applying Pythagoras, the hypotenuse $d^2 = (x_2-x_1)^2 + (y_2-y_1)^2$. The actual distance d is given by the square root of the right-hand side.

Note that you can reverse the order of the x_2 and x_1 as long as you are consistent and reverse the order of the y_2 and y_1 also.

Quadratic Equations and Parabolas

Quadratic equations are the second most important topic in algebra, and you need to understand them well. Linear equations were the first step.

When the highest exponent in an equation is two, as in $y = ax^2+bx+c$, the equation is quadratic, and normally there are two solutions to the equation. This means that there will be two values of x that will solve the quadratic equation.

The two points where the curve cuts the x-axis are the solutions to the quadratic equation (because here y=0). If the curve does not cut the x-axis, there are no solutions, and the solutions are said to be imaginary or complex. If there is only one solution, then the equation is a perfect square, for example, $y = (x+2)^2$, and the curve touches the x-axis at only one point, where x=-2.

The graph of a quadratic equation is a parabola, varying in shape and location. It is concave up if the coefficient a in the equation above is positive, and concave down if a is negative. Use your graphing calculator to plot $y = 2x^2-3x-5$, then change the 2 to -2 and see what happens to the parabola. It flips over!

Note: The later section on Transformations discusses parabolas in greater detail.

Factoring Quadratic Equations

Schools place a lot of emphasis on solving quadratic equations by factoring. This is a vital skill the student must possess since factoring appears several times on a math test. Given an equation like $x^2-2x-3 = 0$, he or she should be able to factor it into $(x-3)(x+1) = 0$ almost immediately.

Factoring is the reverse process of F-O-I-L-ing, which most students know. First-Outside-Inside-Last. This gets rid of the brackets. Factoring brings them back!

Factoring requires a lot of practice, and not all quadratics can be factored. When factorization is not possible, the student will have to use the quadratic formula below, which works in all circumstances.

The Quadratic Formula

Almost all quadratic equations of the type $ax^2+bx+c = 0$ can be solved by using the so-called quadratic formula below:

$$x = \frac{-b \pm \sqrt{b^2 - 4ac}}{2a}$$

As you can imagine, the expression under the radical sign (known as the discriminant) can be positive, negative, or zero. If it is positive or zero, the solutions to the equation are real and straightforward. If the discriminant is negative, the radical does not have a real solution, and the roots to the quadratic equation are said to be complex or imaginary.

Using the quadratic formula usually requires more work, and an easier approach is to make y=0 and then try to factor the expression first. For example, the equation $x^2+3x-4 = 0$ would factor into $(x-1)(x+4) = 0$, so that the roots (or solutions) of the equation are +1 and -4. (Why is this so? If the product of two factors is equal to 0, as above, one or both factors have to equal zero, so that x-1=0, or x+4=0, or both.)

Also, given $x^2+3x-4 = 0$, as above, a=1, b=3 and c=-4. Plugging these values into the quadratic formula above, you will see that x=1 and -4 again.

Note: Questions about slopes and intercepts for linear equations, and about roots or solutions for quadratic equations (both real and imaginary) appear all the time on the SAT and ACT tests, and constitute a majority of the problems. Understanding these concepts well will enable the student to have a good foundation for the tests.

Sum of Roots and Product of Roots

Many problems on both tests are based on quadratic equations, and as you know, these are defined by the equation $ax^2+bx+c = 0$. This equation always has two real or imaginary solutions or roots. Let's call them alpha α and beta β.

It will help the student, and save a lot of time in the test, to remember that the sum of the two roots of this quadratic equation $(\alpha+\beta)$ is equal to the coefficient $-b$ (minus b) above, and the product of the roots $\alpha\beta$ is equal to the coefficient c.

As an example, consider the equation $x^2-3x-10 = 0$. This equation can be factored into $(x+2)(x-5) = 0$. The roots are -2 and 5. The sum of the roots is therefore +3, and the product of the roots is -10. Note that b in this equation is -3 and c is -10.

If there had been a number a before x^2, say 2, as in $2x^2-3x-5=0$, first divide everything by 2 to make a=1. The equation becomes $x^2-\frac{3}{2}x-\frac{5}{2}=0$. The sum of the roots is $+\frac{3}{2}$, and the product is $-\frac{5}{2}$.

Factor Theorem and Remainder Theorem

The number 9 is a factor of 72 since 9 divides 72 exactly, without a remainder.

What is the remainder when 63 is divided by 6? The answer is 3.

Let me now explain to you in a nutshell what the Factor and Remainder Theorems are in algebra since they pop up regularly on the tests. The two theorems are interrelated.

Is (x-2) a factor of x^2+x-6? One way to answer this is to factor the expression or do a long division. The other is to use the Factor Theorem and plug in x=2 in the expression x^2+x-6. If the value becomes zero, there is no remainder, and x-2 is a factor.

Again, is (x+2) a factor of the same expression above? Here you would make x+2=0 and plug in x= -2 in the expression. Now the answer is not zero, so x+2 is not a factor of x^2+x-6. The answer instead is -4, and this is the remainder. Hence, the Remainder Theorem! (The student can verify this by doing a synthetic or long division.)

Direct and Indirect Variation

On the tests, Variation occurs when one variable is connected to another in a relatively simple relationship. For example, $y = kx$, where k is a constant or fixed number.

In a direct relationship, y will increase when x increases, as above. Conversely, when x decreases, y will decrease since k is constant.

With indirect variation, the equation changes to $xy = k$ (or, $y = \frac{k}{x}$) where k is also a constant but has a different value than before. Here, please note that when x increases, y will decrease since k is fixed. Again, if x decreases, y will increase. This is known as inverse or indirect variation.

In variation problems, you are usually given one set of numerical values for x and y (or more variables) so that you can determine the value of the constant, k. Once k is known and you have the full equation, you can always determine the value of any one missing variable, whether x or y, etc. Sometimes, with more difficult problems on the tests, the student may have to set up two equations separately.

Ratios and Proportions

Students sometimes use ratios and proportions recklessly. They realize that it may be a proportion problem and simply put one number on top of another without considering the logic of the situation. Quite often, the proportion is reversed.

For example, if 3 inches on a map represents 8 miles, how much would 5 inches be in reality? The answer is 13.3 miles and not 1.875 miles. (Since 5 is more than 3, the distance should be greater than 8, not less.)

The correct proportion is set up as $\frac{3}{5} = \frac{8}{x}$, so that x=13.3 miles.

With students, I avoid the proportionate method and recommend the 'unit' method below, which is helpful in other situations as well. It is a two-step process and entirely logical: If 3 inches represents 8 miles, then how much does 1 inch (the unit) represent? Next, how much would 5 inches represent? The answer is $\frac{8}{3}$ x 5=13.3 miles, as before.

The Unit Method
The unit method is also useful in situations such as the following:
If it takes John 3 hours to complete a particular project and it takes Susan 4 hours to carry out the same task working alone, how long would it take them to finish the same job working together?

Here the unit method is totally appropriate. In 1 hour (the unit) John can complete 1/3rd of the job, and Susan working alone can accomplish 1/4th of the job. Working together, in one hour, they will finish ($\frac{1}{3}+\frac{1}{4}$), or $\frac{7}{12}$th of the task. In other words, they can finish the task together in $\frac{12}{7}$ or $1\frac{5}{7}$ hours, which is less than 2 hours.

Averages
Problems on simple averages frequently appear on the SAT and ACT tests and, surprisingly, seem to give some students trouble.

Consider, for example, a classroom with 15 boys and 10 girls and an average math score for the whole class of 83, with the average for the boys being 85. What is the average score for the girls? Try it yourself first.

The answer is 80.

Always remember that an average is calculated by dividing the total by the number of observations. Or, Average = $\frac{Sum}{Number}$. Stated differently, the sum or total scores = average x number of students.

Total scores for the classroom are 83x25 = 2075. The total score for the boys is 85 x15 = 1275. Thus, the total score for girls is 2075-1275 = 800. So the average score for the girls is $\frac{800}{10}$ = 80. Simple!

Hence, the key is to use the average to determine the sum first.

Distance, Speed and Time
Anyone who drives a car knows that the distance traveled is equal to the average speed of the car multiplied by the time traveled or,

D=SxT. From this, one can also say that average speed is equal to the distance divided by the time traveled, or the time taken is the distance divided by the speed. Or, $S=\frac{D}{T}$ and $T=\frac{D}{S}$.

Distance, speed, and time problems often appear on the tests and look deceptively simple, such that even good students can go wrong. For example, if half of an (unspecified) distance d is traveled at 30 miles per hour and the remaining half at 50 mph, what is the average speed for the whole journey? You might be tempted to say 40 mph, but you would be wrong. The correct answer is 37.5 mph!

Don't believe me? Take a distance of say 300 miles. Time taken to travel the first 150 miles is 5 hours, and 3 hours for the second half. The total time taken is 8 hours, so the average speed must be 300/8 = 37.5 mph. Happy now?

With these D-S-T problems, it helps to sketch a horizontal distance line and divide it into the relevant parts. In this case, two halves. Then, figure out the time and average speed for each interval separately. Define 'x' to be what the problem is looking for, or thereabout; build an equation with x and solve.

Percentages

It always surprises me when a student has difficulty with percentage problems. They usually understand ratios and proportions but come unstuck on percentages. Why?

If 5 out of 25 students have blonde hair, then the proportion of students with blonde hair is 1 in 5, or the ratio of blonde to other-hair students is 1:4. A percentage is calculated on the assumption that the group size is 100, in which case 20 students would have blonde hair, and the percentage is 20%.

Just remember that percent means "per cent", or one part in a hundred. For example, 8% means 8 parts in 100.

Percentages are necessary to compare two or more groups of different sizes. For example, you cannot directly compare a group of 25 students with another group of 40 students. You need 100 students in each group before comparing.

Percentage problems frequently occur in both tests in different scenarios, and all the time in daily life.

Always be careful about defining the initial or base figure on which the percentage increase or decrease is calculated.

Consider, for example, a small town with a population of 5000 people. The population increases by 20% in the first year and declines by 10% in the second year. What is the overall percentage change in the population over 2 years? The answer is not up 10%! It is 8%, because the decline in the second year is based on the increased population of 6000 at the end of the first year, 5000x1.2= 6000. (Please note that 1.2 represents an increase of 20%, and 0.9 implies a decrease of 10%).

Often when working with percentage problems, as in the last example, it helps to start with 100 and work with the percentage figures directly. My shortcut, using the calculator, would be 100x1.2x0.9=108, which means an increase of 8 on 100 over 2 years.

Drawing a timeline first in this and similar situations is easy and certainly helps to identify the different time periods.

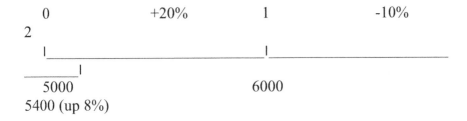

| 0 | +20% | 1 | -10% |
| 2 | | | |

5000
5400 (up 8%)   6000

Functions

Functions are denoted by f(x), where x is the independent variable. For every value of x, there will be a value of f(x). They are an essential part of algebra and repeatedly appear on standardized tests.

Functions could be linear, quadratic, polynomial, or any mathematical expression.

In practice, f(x) replaces the variable y. Instead of writing y=3x+7, we may write f(x) =3x+7. This has two immediate

38

advantages: First, we work with only one variable and not two. Second, if we want the value of the function when x=3, we simply write f(3), which is equal to 16 in this example.

Students have no problem figuring out f(3) above, but the moment you ask them what f(a) is, some get confused. The answer is simply f(a)=3a+7. Just replace the x with the a.

A common reaction with students is that they don't know what f(a) is because they do not know the value of 'a'! Right now, the value of a does not matter and could be anything.

Again, to make it more confusing, I could ask the student what is f(x+z) equal to? The answer is 3(x+z)-7. Merely replace the x with (x+z). OK?

Rational Expressions

Suppose that you are given the equation $\frac{x}{3} + \frac{2}{5} = \frac{5}{8}$ and told to solve for x.

In doing this, I shall explain three essential techniques in algebra which the student should be fluent with and always use. First, he or she should bring all the numbers on one side and leave the variable on the other side. Next, we need to merge or simplify the right-hand side by finding the lowest common denominator (LCD), which in this case is 40.

The equation becomes $\frac{x}{3} = \frac{5}{8} - \frac{2}{5}$, then $\frac{x}{3} = \frac{25-16}{40}$, or $\frac{x}{3} = \frac{9}{40}$. Next, cross-multiply so that $40x = 27$ and divide both sides by 40, so that $x = \frac{27}{40}$.

Rational expressions in algebra are equations involving fractions such as the one below. They are analogous to what we just solved.

$$\frac{3}{x} + \frac{2+x}{x-2} + \frac{12}{15} = \frac{34}{5}$$

This equation, while complicated, should be solved in exactly the same 3-step process as in the previous example. First, bring the numbers to the right-hand side, leaving the variable x on the other

side. Then merge the left-hand side using the lowest common denominator of $x(x-2)$. You will have:
$$\frac{3x-6+2x+x^2}{x(x-2)} = \frac{102-12}{15}$$

Next, cross-multiply and bring all terms on to the left-hand side and make them equal to zero. Factor the left-hand side and find the answers, which are x= 3 or $\frac{2}{5}$.

Finally, make sure both answers work in the original equation, and neither makes the answer undefined and is therefore exogenous.

Practical tip in algebra: Please note that when I move or drag a variable or number from one side of an equation to another (left to right or vice versa), I simply change the sign from + to -, or – to +, as necessary. It is convenient and saves me a lot of time.

Exponents, radicals, etc.

We all know what x^3 means? But, do we know what $\sqrt{x}$ or $x^{1/3}$ or x^{-1} means?

If you know what $x^{-1/2}$ is already, then you are familiar with exponents. It means $\frac{1}{\sqrt{x}}$.

What is x^3 multiplied by x^2? The answer is x^5. You add the exponents because x^3 consists of 3 x's and x^2 consists of 2 x's, making a total of 5 x's, or x^5.

What if I asked you what $(x^3)^2$ is? The answer this time is x^6 because you now have 3 x's in the brackets and the brackets are repeated twice because of the square, making a total of 6 x's.

If you get confused between adding or multiplying, always count the total number of x's involved ultimately, and you will not go wrong.

The same logic will tell you that if you are multiplying powers, you add the exponents, and if you are dividing, you subtract the exponents. For example, $\frac{x^5}{x^3}= x^2$.

A square root or radical sign is a fractional exponent of ½, and a cube root is 1/3. The same rules apply to fractional exponents as to integers: You add exponents when multiplying and you subtract when dividing.

Please remember that a negative exponent is not negative in the standard sense and simply represents a reciprocal. For example, x^{-2} means $1/x^2$.

A negative exponent in the numerator of an expression becomes positive when transferred to the denominator, and vice versa. That is, a negative exponent in the denominator becomes positive when transferred to the numerator.

To simplify complicated expressions with many variables and exponents, start by eliminating all the parentheses first; next turn all negative exponents into positive exponents by taking them from the numerator into the denominator, or the other way round as necessary, and simplify as much as possible. These problems require a fair amount of practice to do correctly.

As an example, what is $\sqrt[3]{54x^5}$ equal to? To do this, break up both components into prime factors and take triplets out because it is a cube root. Here, x^5 is x.x.x.x.x. There is one set of triplets involved, so take one x outside the radical and leave x^2 within the radical. Similarly, 54=3.3.3.2. Take one 3 out and leave the 2 under the radical sign. The answer is $3x\sqrt[3]{2x^2}$.

If you had a square root, you would look for twins. With a fourth root, you would seek quadruplets!

Arithmetic and Geometric Series

A sequence such as 3,5,7,9...........31 is an Arithmetic Series and involves the constant <u>addition</u> of a fixed number to the previous number. The common difference here is 2.

There are 15 terms in the series above. To find the 15th term, you would take the first term and add the constant difference of 2 fourteen times (one less than 15) to make a total of 31.

To sum these 15 terms, find the average of the first and last term and multiply by the number of terms. The average of the first and last term is equal to $(3+31)/2 = 17$. The sum of this series is, therefore, $17 \times 15 = 255$.

An arithmetic series is easy to identify since the difference between successive terms is always the same, whether positive or negative. For example, 27, 24, 21, 18, 15. 12, 9 is also an arithmetic series of 7 terms with a common difference of negative 3.

It is useful to remember that the series, in general terms, is stated as a, a+d, a+2d,......a+(n-1)d, where d could be positive or negative. Note that the nth term is equal to [a+(n-1)d].

A Geometric Series involves <u>multiplication</u> and, for example, is given by 3,6,12,24,48 ...... where each previous term is multiplied by 2. The 15th term is huge, and in the test, you will not be asked to add this series.

Here the factor of 2 you used to multiply the previous term is called the common 'ratio' and is usually denoted by 'r'.

In general terms, the series is: a, ar, ar^2, ar^3 .... $ar^{(n-1)}$, where 'a' is the initial term, and 'r' is the common ratio.

Most geometric series cannot be added (beyond a few terms) because each successive term becomes bigger and bigger and ultimately approaches infinity. These series are known as 'divergent'.

If a specific geometric series is 'convergent', such as $2, 1, \frac{1}{2}, \frac{1}{4}$ ...., with a common ratio of say $\frac{1}{2}$, it can be added to infinity and the sum is given by $S = \frac{a}{1-r}$, where a is the first term. Here the sum to infinity is equal to $\frac{2}{(1-\frac{1}{2})} = 4$. The student should remember this simple formula for the tests.

A geometric series can normally be added for a specific number of consecutive terms, but the formula is complicated, and I have yet to see this type of problem in the tests.

Believe it or not, this may be all the student needs to know of these two types of series for the standardized tests.

<u>Conics: Circles, Parabolas, Ellipses & Hyperbolas</u>

If you take an inverted cone and slice it horizontally, you will get a perfect circle. If you cut the cone at an angle and go through the base, you will have a parabola. If you go through two sides of a cone, you have an ellipse. Finally, for a hyperbola, you need to slice two cones together vertically, with one cone inverted on top of another, in the shape of an hourglass. Hence, the name 'conics'!

Circles: Some 2500 years ago, the Greeks figured out that the ratio between the circumference of a circle and its diameter was always constant regardless of the size of the circle, and they decided to call the ratio 'pi' or π. They then came up with two of the most celebrated formulas in basic math for the circumference and the area of a circle: $C=\pi d$ or $C=2\pi r$ and $A=\pi r^2$, where d is the diameter and r is the radius of the circle.

Those who have difficulty remembering these formulas should think "Cherry pie delicious" for $C=\pi d$, and "Apple pies are too!" for $A=\pi r^2$. These formulas are given to you in SAT, but not in the ACT test.

You should know the basic equation of a circle with its center at the origin (0,0). This is a simple use of The Pythagorean Theorem. Sketch any circle and draw a radius to a point (x,y) on the circumference. Next, draw the x and y-coordinates for that point and connect the three sides of the triangle, with the radius as the third side. You now have a right-angled triangle and can write the equation of the circle, using Pythagoras, as $x^2+y^2 = r^2$, with the radius r as the hypotenuse of the triangle.

When the center of the circle above is moved from the origin to a point (h, k) elsewhere on the chart, Pythagoras still applies, and the generalized equation of the circle becomes the following:
$$(x-h)^2 + (y-k)^2 = r^2$$
The student should also remember this equation because questions will be based on it in the SAT and ACT tests, and this equation will not be provided.

Again, he or she may be given a general equation like $x^2+y^2-4x-6y = 3$ and asked to figure out the radius of the circle. To do this, the student will need to complete two perfect squares and transform the equation into the general form given above.

I assume that you remember how to complete a square. For example, if you are given $x^2 -4x$ (as above) and asked to complete the square, you will add a 4 and simultaneously subtract a 4, so that the expression becomes $(x^2-4x+4)-4$. This can now be written as $(x-2)^2-4$, and the first part is a perfect square! Do the same with the second variable y so that you have $(y-3)^2 -9$. Add these two parts together and you will end up with the equation $(x-2)^2+(y-$

3)²=3+4+9=16. The right-hand side gives you the square of the radius, which is therefore 4.

Ellipses are either flattened or elongated circles, also with their centers either at the origin or elsewhere. You should memorize their formulas below, where 'a' and 'b' represent <u>one-half</u> of the major and minor axes respectively. (Major and minor axes are the maximum and minimum diameters of the ellipse, respectively.)

$\dfrac{x^2}{a^2} + \dfrac{y^2}{b^2} = 1$, with center at (0,0)

If both are equal, and a=b, the figure becomes a circle with equation $x^2 + y^2 = r^2$.

When the center is shifted away from the origin, the ellipse is represented by the formula $\dfrac{(x-h)^2}{a^2} + \dfrac{(y-k)^2}{b^2} = 1$, with center at (h,k).

With **hyperbolas**, which sometimes appear in the math test, just remember that the positive sign in the formula for ellipses changes to a negative, as shown below, but the graph changes dramatically. (Try plotting the two curves on your calculator with a=2 and b=3, first with the positive sign and then with the negative, and you will see the striking difference.)

$\dfrac{x^2}{a^2} - \dfrac{y^2}{b^2} = 1$, with center at (0,0)

You should know what the 'focus' of an ellipse or hyperbola means, but don't worry too much about definitions such as directrix, latus rectum, etc. They are difficult to remember, and at most, the student will have one question on them in the test.

Logarithms

In the old days, when there were no electronic or manual calculators, we still had to do problems like 3478 x 792. Multiplications or long divisions took a long time, so logarithms were created, and we could get approximate results fairly quickly.

Logarithms convert multiplication problems into addition and division into subtraction, which is vastly easier. Let's take a simple problem to make the point. Multiply 16 by 8. 16 can be written as 2^4

44

and 8 as 2^3. To multiply 2^4 and 2^3, you add the two exponents 4 and 3 together to yield 2^7. An "anti-log" table would tell you that the answer is 128. In real life, we do not use the base of 2 but common logs with a base of 10. (Just remember that in common logs 1,000, for example, would be written as 10^3.)

Now that electronic calculators are available, we do not need logarithms for such basic calculation purposes, but we still need them for other reasons. Consider, for example, how you would calculate the time it would take to triple your $1000 investment at 8% interest. Here we would still use logs and write $1000(1.08)^x = 3000$, or $(1.08)^x = 3$, where x is equal to the time it would take to triple the money. Using common logs with base 10, we would write this as x log 1.08 = log 3. Using log tables, solve $x = \dfrac{\log 3}{\log 1.08}$, so that x=14.27 years.

The student should always be able to convert exponents to logs and vice versa. $10^3 = 1000$, so 3 is the log of 1000 to the base 10. Or, $2^5 = 32$, so 5 is the log of 32 to the base 2. This is written as $\log_2 32 = 5$.

If you are familiar with exponents, you will be able to handle logs easily. Here are some rules to remember:

To multiply two numbers, you add the logs. For example, if AB=C, then log A + log B=log C.

Similarly, to divide, you subtract. That is, log (D/E) = log D - log E.

A complicated expression like $\log (2x^2y^3/z^5) =$ log2+2logx+3logy-5logz

The square root of x or $\sqrt{x}$ would be written in logarithm as ½ log x, and this is how you will deal with fractional or negative exponents.

While the basic rules are straightforward, some of the problems given in the tests with logs can be difficult, so practice is essential.

In some problems, the student may have to change the base of a log. If so, look in a textbook for the change of base formula, but this is not a common question.

Similar Triangles
Problems on similar triangles are common on the tests.

If the three angles of one triangle are equal to the three angles of a second triangle, the two triangles are said to be similar.

We all know that the three angles of any triangle together add up to 180°. Therefore, if any two angles of a triangle are each equal to two angles of another triangle, the third angles will also be equal.

If two triangles are similar, it does not mean that they have the same size. They have the same shape but the sides normally are of different sizes.

Figure out the ratio of two corresponding sides of similar triangles, and the third sides will also be in the same ratio. For example, if two triangles are similar and one side is three times as big as the corresponding side of the second triangle, then all three sides will be in the ratio of 3:1.

On the tests, it is important to know (and many students do not realize this) that the area of the first triangle in the example above will be 9 times as big as the area of the second triangle. This is because area = $\frac{1}{2}$ base x height and 3 x 3 = 9. Again, if the sides of one triangle are five times as big as another similar triangle, the area will be 25 times as large!

Solid Geometry - Volumes

Instead of trying to memorize various formulas, just realize that the volume of a rectangular solid is simply the area of the base of the solid multiplied by the vertical height of the solid. Since the area of the base is length x width and h is the height, the volume of a rectangular solid is given by V= l w h.

Similarly, the volume of a cylinder is the area of its circular base multiplied by its height. The area of the circular base is πr^2, where r is the radius. If the height is h, the volume of the cylinder is given by V=πr^2h.

If a solid figure is a triangular prism (shaped like a rectangular tent), try turning the solid figure on its side so that the triangular side becomes the base, and the length of the prism becomes the vertical height. Then, as earlier, the volume of the prism is the area of the base triangle multiplied by the height.

Volume of a vertical cone?

By some natural law, the volume of a vertical cone is always one-third of the volume of the corresponding cylinder. Volume of a cone,

$V = \frac{1}{3}\pi r^2 h$.

Volume of a vertical pyramid?

Again, the volume of a square or rectangular pyramid is one-third of the area of the base multiplied by the vertical height. $V = \frac{1}{3} l\ w\ h$.

Volume of a sphere?

Finally, the volume of a sphere with radius r is difficult to explain or remember. It is Volume$= \frac{4}{3}\pi r^3$, and the formula is usually provided to the student in the test when needed.

Solid Geometry-Surface Areas

For surface areas, we have to calculate the area of each face of the solid figure and add them together. For example, the surface area of a cube is the sum of the areas of six equal faces, each with side s and area s^2, for a total surface area of $6s^2$.

Similarly, the total surface area of a rectangular solid is double the three equal and opposite faces, or 2(lw+lh+wh), where l, w, and h represent the length, width, and height of the rectangular solid respectively.

A standard prism or pyramid has 5 faces. A cylinder has 3 faces, with a circular base and a circular top, and a cylindrical vertical surface which opens out into a rectangular surface.

A cone has two surfaces: a circular base with radius r and area πr^2, and a lateral area which, when opened out, has an area analogous to a triangle with a curved base. The length of the curved base is equal to the circumference of the circular base of the cone, or $2\pi r$. The height of the so-called triangle is the slant height, not the vertical height. Since the area of a triangle is ½ x base x height, the lateral surface area is ½ .2πr.l, or simply πrl, where l is the slant height.

Solid Geometry - Revolving Solids

These solids are created by rotating a two-dimensional figures, such as a rectangle or a triangle, around the x- or y-axis. A rectangle rotated around the y-axis would produce a cylinder. A right-angle triangle, when rotated on one leg about the x-axis, would produce a horizontal cone. When rotated on the other leg about the y-axis, there would be a vertical cone.

Revolving solid figures appear in the math subject tests, Levels 1 & 2, and typically not in the regular tests because they can be hard!

Complex numbers

We all know the square root of radical 100. It is 10. However, what is the square root of -100, or $\sqrt{-100}$? Many students answer -10, but this cannot be true since -10 multiplied by -10 is equal to +100, not -100. H is where imaginary numbers come in.

The lowercase 'i' is defined as equal to the square root of negative one. This is a definition, so $i = \sqrt{-1}$. Believe it or not, this makes it possible to find the roots of negative numbers!

Consider, for example, -100 above. This can now be written as the product of +100 and -1. Therefore, the square root of -100 is equal to the square root of +100 multiplied by the square root of -1. The former is 10, and the latter is defined as 'i', so the answer is 10i. Hence, $\sqrt{-100}$ is equal to 10i. Brilliant!

10 is a real number like all other numbers in general use. 'i' is an imaginary or complex number, so the product 10i is imaginary.

Another example: what is the square root of -72? The answer is 6i $\sqrt{2}$.

Most complex numbers can be written as part real and part imaginary, or A+Bi, where A and B are both real numbers, but Bi is imaginary.

There is much more on the subject of complex or imaginary numbers later.

Some Difficult Problem Types in the Tests

Always focus on what the problem is asking

Word Problems

Students commonly have difficulty with word problems. These problems describe a real-life situation and ask you for the answer to a specific question.

For example, the problem may say that there are 800 students in a school with three times as many boys as girls. How many girls are there?

Students read more detailed versions of this kind of problem and are often confused because they don't know where to start. The starting point is critically important. If you don't know where or how to start, you will not be able to solve the word problem.

The key is to focus on precisely what the problem is asking you for. Here, you will focus on the total number of girls in the school.

I then say to the student: Since you do not know how many girls there are, tell yourself you will call the number of girls 'x'. Given the number of girls as x, the total number of boys will be 3x. All you need now is to build one equation in x, based on the information provided in the problem. Here x+3x=800. Solving, you get that x=200, so the total number of girls in the school is 200.

There will always be enough information in the question to form one equation. Once you solve this equation, you will know x and have the answer to the problem. Sometimes, you may have to tweak the value of x a little bit to get to the exact answer required.

On occasion, it may be easier to use two variables x and y to solve the problem. You will then need to form two equations from the data provided and solve them simultaneously. Here y = 3x and x + y= 800, where y = total number of boys in the school and x is as before.

If you have enough time during the test, you should quickly check your answer to make sure that it makes sense. Plug your answer back into the original word problem to see that it works.

Problems are not always as easy as the one above. If at any time you do not comprehend a problem, read it again and again. Try breaking it down into smaller bits which are understandable, and then link them together to make sense. I say to students: do not try to swallow the problem whole, as a python would its prey! Instead, chew the problem bit by bit and stay alive.

Roman Numerals Problems

You might have seen various math test problems which use Roman numerals I, II, and III to define various alternative situations. The multiple-choice answers list different combinations of the Roman numerals as being the correct answer. These can be among the most difficult types of problems on the test. Fortunately, they do not occur more than once or twice in a test.

When I first started teaching, I used to look at the alternatives and choose one multiple-choice answer based on my best judgment. I found that I was wrong nearly half the times. This approach is a natural way and most students use it intuitively, but it does not always work well.

A more efficient approach, I discovered, is to think of the problem as three separate problems. Look at the first alternative (I) and say to yourself: Is this answer by itself true or false; or, respond yes or no? Note down the answer.

Do this for the second alternative II and write down true or false again or, if you prefer, yes or no. Repeat this for the third alternative III.

Having done this separately three times, then combine the answers and choose the right multiple-choice answer.

If you take this longer route to solve the problem, you will find that you will be right much more often. Good luck!

Symbol Problems

These symbol problems occur less often in the new SAT than before, but continue as earlier with the ACT. These are not typical classroom problems and are often intimidating to students.

When a student sees a symbol (such as a club, spade, cloverleaf, horseshoe, sunflower, or anything else) in a mathematical equation, they throw up their hands in alarm and say that they do not know what it means! I calm them down by saying that neither do I!

When a foreign object or symbol is introduced into a mathematical expression or equation, only the authorities who constructed the problem know what it represents. They have to tell us what the object stands for or means before anyone can answer the problem.

I tell the student that a new symbol always has to be defined exactly – otherwise, no one can deal with the problem. For example, Ω may be defined as equal to $x(x-3)$, or $\Omega = x(x-3)$. What then is the value of $3\Omega-7$ when $x=5$? You simply replace the symbol with x's and plug in 5 to get a numerical value. $3x(x-3)-7 = 3.5(5-3)-7 = 23$.

The key in all this is to follow the definition exactly as given, and the whole problem becomes manageable.

As I said earlier, they have reduced the frequency of these types of problems in the SAT, presumably because they are not taught in the classroom.

Transformations

Knowing transformations well will help you in understanding what is really happening in several common situations in algebra, geometry, or trigonometry.

Transformations deal with changes to the underlying (or generic) equation of any line or curve. You can take a curve and move it up or down; sideways to the left or right; squish or flatten the curve (that is, compress or stretch it), or simply reflect it across the x-axis or y-axis.

A rectangular coordinate plane is comprised of an x-axis and a y-axis, defining four quadrants I, II, III, and IV in a counterclockwise fashion, starting with the top right quadrant. Any equation in x and y defines a line or curve on this plane, for example, a line $y = mx+b$, or a parabola, defined by $f(x) = ax^2+bx+c$:

Vertical shifts: If you add a positive number, say 4, to the function $f(x)$ to make it $f(x)+4$, it will produce a vertical shift of the whole curve up by 4. Similarly, $f(x)-4$ would shift the original curve down by 4.

Horizontal shifts: Subtracting a number inside the brackets to make it $f(x-4)$ would produce a horizontal shift to the right-hand side. Since the number is negative, note that the move is to the positive side and is therefore counterintuitive. A +4 inside the parenthesis would produce a shift to the left, or the negative side.

A ***Multiplier*** either squishes or flattens a curve, making it narrower or flatter. A number greater than one multiplied by f(x) would increase the slope of the curve and cause it to rise faster. For example, the parabola 3f(x) would be narrower than the original curve f(x). A number less than 1 would flatten the curve since it will have a lower slope and rise slower.

Reflection: If you put a minus sign in front of the function, it will flip or rotate the entire curve around the x-axis. In other words, it will end up being concave down instead of concave up (convex), or vice versa.

Similarly, you can reflect a curve around the y-axis by replacing x with −x.

Generic Curves: If you know the generic (or parent) forms of standard curves, you will be able to draw almost any curve by making the necessary transformations.

For example, the generic of a linear graph is simply y=x passing through the origin (0,0) at 45 degrees angle. In order to draw y=3x+7, you will do a vertical shift up of 7 first and then increase the slope to 3 so that the line rises more sharply. (A slope of 3 means a rise of three for a run of one.) The y-intercept is now +7 and the line has a positive slope of 3.

Now, let's say that you wish to draw the parabola $f(x) = 2x^2 - 4x + 5$. You would first have to do a little algebraic manipulation (i.e., completing squares) to rewrite the function as $f(x) = 2(x-1)^2 + 3$ since this would clearly display the transformations required. Start with the generic curve for a parabola of $y=x^2$, passing through the origin. First, do a counterintuitive, horizontal shift to the right of 1, since -1 appears inside the brackets and modifies the x. Next, narrow or squish the curve to make it rise twice as fast. Finally, shift the entire curve vertically upwards by 3, and you now have your final product, the required curve!

Parabolas, or quadratic equations, are an important part of high school math. If you can do these transformations yourself, starting with the generic curve, it will take you a long way in better understanding x- and y-intercepts, zeros, axis of symmetry, vertex, maxima and minima, etc. - a whole lot, and it doesn't take that long!

Probability

If you ask the typical math student which topic he or she finds most difficult in the SAT and ACT tests, the response is likely to be Probability. This is not surprising since probability can be hard and confusing. However, you only need a basic understanding of the topic for the tests.

First, learn to differentiate between **Permutations and Combinations**. With permutations, the order of selection matters; with combinations, the order does not matter. For example, if you have a club with 12 members and you wish to choose a President, Vice President and Treasurer, how many different ways can you make the selection? Here, the order matters and this is a permutation problem. Let's start with the President: you can choose him or her in 12 ways since there are 12 members. Next, you can fill the position of Vice President in 11 ways since one member has already been taken as President. Likewise, the Secretary can be chosen in 10 ways since 2 members were selected previously. The total number of different ways in which the selection of all three positions can be made is therefore 12x11x10=1320.

For a combination example, let's take the same club with 12 members and now think of sending exactly 3 members to Paris to attend a seminar. How many different ways can you choose who goes to Paris? Here, the order does not matter, since the order in which the three members board the plane is not relevant. Here, you will take the previous answer to the permutation problem and cut out all possible duplications since the order does not now matter. This is like saying that BAC is the same as CBA or ABC, since the order does not matter. Since you can permute 3 members in 6 different ways, you will take the previous answer of 1320 and divide it by 6 to give you the required number of combinations of 220.

Probabilities are said to be 'independent' when the likelihood or chance of an event occurring does not depend on the outcome of a prior event. If the outcome of an event impacts the likelihood of another event, the probabilities are dependent.

With **successive events**, you are going to be multiplying independent probabilities. For example, if the likelihood of rain on any one day is constant at $\frac{1}{4}$, the combined probability of rain on all three days is going to be 1/4 x1/4x1/4=1/64. Again, the probability that it will not rain on any of the three days is the product of 3/4x3/4x3/4=27/64.

There are, of course, other probabilities for rain on some days and not the others. For example, what is the likelihood that it will rain at least one day (37/64) or exactly two days (9/64)?

When events are not successive, but **simultaneous,** the probabilities are additive. Assume that there are only three possibilities for the weather on any one day: sun, snow, or rain, each with its own probability. Here, the events are not successive and probabilities should be added (not multiplied) and the total would not exceed unity, or one. Thus, if each of the three weather conditions is equally likely, the likelihood of snow today is 1/3 and the probability of snow and rain together is 2/3 (not 1/9).

A third, most common way of calculating probabilities in different situations is to compute the total number of **favorable outcomes** (either permutations or combinations) and dividing it by the corresponding total number of possible outcomes. "Favorable" means those which comply with the conditions or parameters stated in the problem. For example, if there are 5 table tennis players, with 3 men and 2 women, and you have to select a team of two players at random, what is the likelihood that you would end up with 1 man and 1 woman. Answer: The number of favorable ways is 3x2=6 and the total number of ways is a combination of 2 out of 5, equal to (5x4)/2=10. The final probability is the favorable outcomes divided by the total number of outcomes, given by 6/10, and equal to 3/5 or 60%.

The numerical value of a probability can only be between 0 and 1, with both extremes inclusive. 1 means certainty and 0 means not going to happen.

Inequalities

Inequalities can be in one or two variables. One-variable inequalities are easy enough to solve, and the answer will also be an inequality. For example, given 3x-8<4, you would bring the numbers to the right hand side and divide by 3, so that the answer is x<4.

With two variables, x and y, the situation is complicated, as follows:

An equation like y=3x+8 describes a straight line with a slope of 3 and a y-intercept of 8. An inequality like y<3x+8 represents the area below the line, but does not include the line itself. If the equality sign had been included, as in $y \leq 3x + 8$, then the line would also be included in the area.

The student may be given two different inequalities and asked to find their solution, as follows:

The second inequality would define a second line and a second area either below or above the line, depending on the direction of the inequality sign.

The area common to both inequalities, if it exists, would define the solution to the two inequalities. The answer is not one point but many points in the area.

As a separate issue, if you change the sign of an inequality on both sides from minus to plus or vice versa, you have to flip the direction of the inequality. This is intuitive and a common situation. Most students are familiar with this requirement.

A difficult situation arises when the inequality includes an absolute value sign, which, as you know, means that the value cannot be negative. Here you would have to split the inequality into two inequalities, one positive and the other negative. The inequality sign should be flipped in the case of the negative part, and this would produce a V-shaped graph. Then, solve the two inequalities separately in the same manner as single-variable inequalities, and the solution would be the combined range of values.

For example, solve Ix-4I≥ 7. This breaks up into two inequalities x-4≥ 7 and x-4≤ -7. Solving, we get x≥ 11 and x≤ -3, so that the answer lies in two separate regions. (Note that the inequality sign was flipped when 7 was changed to -7).

A specific type of challenging problem in inequalities appears in the tests involving absolute values. For example, the problem may say that x lies between -3 and 7, and asks you which absolute value inequality Ix-3I<4 or Ix-2I<5 correctly represents these values.

You can use trial and error and plug in different numbers to see if they work. However, it is much easier to use the mid-point of the range of x-values given, which in this case is 2, and write your answer as $|x-2|<5$, since 5 is the distance to the end value on either side.

Less Essential Topics (Miscellaneous)

Cross-multiplying always helps

Imaginary Numbers

Imaginary or complex numbers are an esoteric part of high school math, and usually no more than one or two questions on them will appear on any one test. If you are not familiar with this topic and have limited time, you may elect to skip it.

The most important aspect of complex numbers is to understand clearly what i stands for; then i^2, i^3 and i^4. This represents a cycle of four, which repeats itself.

Since $i=\sqrt{-1}$, realize that i^2 will always equal -1. Again, $i^3= i^2 \cdot i = -1$. $i = -i$, and $i^4 = i^2 \cdot i^2 = -1 \cdot -1 = +1$. Because i^4 equals +1, the cycle repeats itself after every four powers.

Let's say that you are asked for the value of i^{22}. You would say that $i^{22}=i^{20} \cdot i^2$. And, i^{20} is five complete cycles of fours, which is equal to +1. The remainder is i^2, which is equal to -1. Hence, $i^{22}=-1$. Makes sense?

A standard problem with complex numbers on tests involving FOIL-ing these numbers to end up with the standard format of A+Bi, where A and B are real numbers, and i is complex. For example, (3-4i)(2+5i)=6+15i-8i-20i², or 6+7i+20=26+7i. Hence, A=26 and B=7 here.

Please note that the A+Bi includes both real and complex numbers. When a number is real, B would be zero. For example, the real number 5 can be written as 5+0.i.

Another standard situation on the tests is the rationalization of the denominator of a complex expression. Here, 'rationalization' means getting rid of the 'i' in the denominator.

The process involves the use of the so-called 'conjugate' and the algebraic identity (a+b)(a-b)= a²-b². For example:

$$\frac{2+3i}{8-3i} = \frac{(2+3i)(8+3i)}{(8-3i)(8+3i)} = \frac{16+30i+9i^2}{64-9i^2}$$

$$= \frac{7+30i}{73}$$

The conjugate of 8-3i is 8+3i, and vice versa. Multiplying conjugates together produces a real number. The product here is 8^2-$(3i)^2 = 64-9(-1)=73$. There is no 'i' in the denominator now.

Proofs and Congruence

Although I have done a lot of tutoring of logic and proofs with high school geometry students, (which is often challenging and tedious), I do not recall seeing proofs on the SAT and ACT tests.

Congruence, however, is a somewhat different story. Any triangle has three sides and three angles, making a total of six elements. If any three components are given to you, then, most of the times, it should be possible to find the other three elements exactly. Also, given two triangles, if it is known that three components of one triangle are equal to three components of the other triangle, it should be mostly possible to establish that the two triangles are congruent. This is the same as proving that the two triangles are equal in every way.

Although congruence, or establishing the equivalence of two triangles, is a relevant and useful subject, I haven't seen many questions on this topic on the tests. Standard theorems to establish congruence, such as Side-Angle-Side or SAS, ASA, HSL and SSS, do not frequently appear on the tests. This could change in the future.

Statistics/Scatterplots/Regression

The new SAT test and the ACT usually include one or more problems on visual and mathematical statistics.

In statistics, you should know clearly the difference between mean (average), mode, and median. Confusion here could cost you a lot of points. Mean is when you add up all the observations or measurements and divide by the total number of observations. Mode is the observation that occurs the most frequently. Median is the middle number that has an equal number of observations, higher and lower, on both sides.

Know what a stem-and-leaf plot is on the tests. It is a shorthand form of writing similar numbers and is easy. Look in a textbook or simply Google it.

Also, understand what the inter-quartile range (IQR) means. Find the median of the entire data first. This is the 50th percentile of the data. Then find two other medians, one on either side of the median. These would be the 25th and 75th percentiles, representing the first and third quartiles, Q1 and Q3, respectively. The difference between these two quartiles is the IQR.

You should know what a scatterplot of raw data represents. It is simply numerical data plotted against a variable on a graph sheet. A scatterplot usually gives you an idea about which type of regression, if any, would best fit the raw data. Use your calculator to do the regression or curve fitting (whether linear, growth, decay, curvilinear, etc.). From the mathematical curve, you can read off estimated values at different points on the curve or project the data for additional (extrapolated) values.

The students should understand 'mean deviation' and the important concept of 'standard deviation'. Both mean and standard deviation measure how closely the data is spread around the mean value. The bigger the number, the more widely the data is dispersed, and vice versa.

Probability density functions are essential in statistics, and the Normal Distribution is the one most commonly used in real life. These do not appear on the regular SAT and ACT yet.

Trigonometry 2

A simple identity in trigonometry is $sin^2x + cos^2x = 1$, which frequently occurs on the tests and should be remembered at all times.

The inverse of a trigonometric function is very different from the inverse of an algebraic function. The latter simply interchanges the x and y and solves for y. The inverse of a trig function is, believe it or not, an angle. For example, sin 30° = ½, and the sine inverse of ½=30 degrees, written as $sin^{-1}\dfrac{1}{2} = 30°$. You need your scientific calculator to determine inverses in trigonometry unless they are the commonly observed angles.

There are many identities and formulas in trigonometry, but you need not worry about them too much right now. However, the Sine Rule and the Cosine Rule do show up on the standardized tests regularly, and you have to know them.

Sine Rule: Draw a triangle ABC and mark the three angles A, B and C in clockwise order. Mark the side opposite angle A as a, and the sides opposite angles B and C as b and c, respectively. Then, the Sine Rule says that $\frac{a}{sinA} = \frac{b}{sinB} = \frac{c}{sinC}$. (Or, you could switch the numerators and denominators.)

With the sides and angles defined the same way as above in a triangle, the **Cosine Rule** says that $a^2 = b^2 + c^2 - 2bc.cosA$. Or, you can interchange the sides and angles so that any one side appears on the left side of the equation and the other two sides with the included angle appear on the right-hand side.

Finally, we all know that the basic formula for the area of a triangle is $A = \frac{1}{2}base.height$. In trigonometry, it is generalized as $A = \frac{1}{2}bc.sinA$, where A, b and c are defined as in previous paragraphs and can be interchanged as before.

Questions sometimes appear on the tests on drawing or interpreting sine and cosine curves. This involves the discussion of amplitude, periods, vertical and phase shifts, maximum and minimum, etc. and is a difficult topic in trigonometry. Please refer to a textbook if you are interested.

If the three sides of a triangle are known, it is possible to determine the area of a triangle, without knowing any angle by using Hero's formula, although I haven't seen it on tests yet. This formula involves using half the perimeter of the triangle and is available in most textbooks.

Identities are an extensive subject in trigonometry but appear only in their basic form on the two standardized tests. Refer to any book for sin (A+B), sin (A-B), and cos (A+B) with cos(A-B). These four are basic and should be remembered. Double angles and half-angles can be derived from them.

Rectangular and Polar Coordinates

Rectangular coordinates are the x- and y-coordinates we are all used to. The system of (x,y) coordinates is not the only way to represent a point on a plane. Polar coordinates (r, θ) would also describe the location of the point on the same plane, based on the length of the radius r and the angle formed between the radius and the horizontal axis. Know the relationships between the two systems: x=rcosθ and y=rsinθ. If you are given polar coordinates, you can always convert them to rectangular coordinates using these relationships and proceed as usual.

(If you are unable to follow this brief introduction, please refer to a textbook.)

Parametric Equations

These equations involve three variables and occur when x is defined as a function of the third variable 't,' and y is also defined as another function of t. For the purpose of the tests, simply eliminate the third variable t algebraically to get a standard equation in x and y, and continue as normal.

For example, if you are given the two parametric equations x=3sint and y=2cost, with t as the parameter, you can square both equations separately to get $sin^2t = \dfrac{x^2}{9}$ and $cos^2t = \dfrac{y^2}{4}$.

Since $sin^2t + cos^2t$=1, then $\dfrac{x^2}{9} + \dfrac{y^2}{4}$ =1, or $\dfrac{x^2}{3^2} + \dfrac{y^2}{2^2}$ =1, which is an equation in x and y only. This happens to be the equation of an ellipse, centered at the origin, with major axis of 3.2=6 and minor axis of 2.2=4.

Vectors

A line has length only but a vector has both magnitude and direction. Vectors rarely appear on the tests and when they do, they are at a basic level.

Know how to break up a vector into its component x- and y-forms so that the vector originates at the origin (0,0) of the graph. On the tests, vectors may be given to you in component form already.

Know how to combine two vectors with different magnitudes and directions into a resultant vector. This is easiest when the two vectors are in component forms. Simply add the x-components together and then the y-components to get the resultant components, thereby the resultant vector.

You could also do this graphically by constructing a parallelogram and using the directions and magnitudes given. The appropriate diagonal would then represent the resultant vector.

Know also how to calculate a unit vector. You would use Pythagoras on the components of a vector to obtain the magnitude of its resultant, and then divide each component by the magnitude to unitize the vector. For example, consider two vectors in component forms, (3,5) and (2,4). The resultant vector is (5,9), and its magnitude is $\sqrt{5^2 + 9^2}$, or $\sqrt{106} = 10.3$. The unitized vector is ($\frac{5}{10.3}, \frac{9}{10.3}$), or (.49, .87).

Determinants and Matrices

Determinants have two rows and two columns and can be handled manually. If a determinant is represented by first rows a, b and second row c, d, the value of the determinant is given by (ad-cb). This is like saying that the value of a determinant is the difference between the downward diagonal product and the upward diagonal product, if you will.

Matrices are an esoteric topic in high school math, and you may omit them if rushed for time. Their main application is in solving equations with three variables x, y, and z, which rarely appear on the two standardized tests.

The key to dealing with higher-order matrices is to always think of them as multiplying Row by Column.

Higher-order matrices are best evaluated using your calculator, so learn how to enter these matrices into your calculator and manipulate them.

The subject of Calculus is based entirely on the concept of Limits. What are limits?

Imagine that you are standing in a room facing a wall. Let's say that you walk half-way to the wall in the shortest distance possible and stop. Then you walk half-way of the remaining distance again to the wall. You do that again, and again, and again ……. You will certainly get closer and closer to the wall, but will you ever reach the wall?

The answer is a resounding no, and the wall is the <u>limit</u> to your walking expedition. Get the idea of limits?

You may have one or more problems on the SAT and ACT on limits. These are relatively simple problems requiring mainly algebra to solve them. Simplify the expression given to you by first factoring the numerator and denominator separately, or rewrite the expression in a different algebraic form. Then plug in the number for the limit, and you will have the answer.

For example, what is the limit of $\dfrac{2x + 1}{x - 1}$ when x approaches infinity? Rewrite the expression as $2 + \dfrac{3}{x - 1}$, which is identical. Now you will see that, as x becomes larger and larger, the right part becomes smaller and smaller; it approaches zero and disappears, yielding a limit of 2. (Note that with the original expression, $\dfrac{\infty}{\infty}$ is indeterminate.)

Asymptotes

Asymptotes utilize the concept of limits and appear on the two tests. A horizontal asymptote, if it exists, is the limit the curve approaches as x becomes larger and larger. Find this value by making x approach infinity on both sides, positive and negative.

For example, find the horizontal asymptote of the expression $\dfrac{x}{x + 1}$. If you plug in infinity for x, the expression will become indeterminable. If you transform the expression algebraically by dividing the top and bottom by x, it becomes $\dfrac{1}{1+\dfrac{1}{x}}$. Now, notice that when x becomes larger and larger, $\dfrac{1}{x}$ becomes smaller and smaller and finally disappears. The limit is therefore 1, and the horizontal asymptote is defined by y=1.

A vertical asymptote goes straight up and occurs when the value of the denominator in the expression becomes zero, and the expression becomes undefined, or DNE. In the example above, the denominator becomes zero when x= -1, because $\dfrac{-1}{0}$ does not exist. The vertical asymptote, therefore, occurs when x=-1 and is represented by that equation. (Note that on a graph of the function, there is no value for y when x=-1.)

Vertical asymptotes are easier to find, and there may be more than one, depending on the original expression.

Precalculus

Precalculus in high school contains a variety of mathematical concepts, including trigonometry. In some ways, precalculus is more difficult than calculus itself because of the diversity of its concepts. Invariably, those students who include precalculus in their curriculum in high school do better on standardized math tests. In this book, I have discussed most of the major topics in precalculus which appear on the SAT or ACT tests.

AP Calculus

The two main areas in calculus are differentiation and integration, and these are based on the concept of limits. Calculus is vital to the development of all science, including problems in engineering, technology, medicine, space, etc. While there is precalculus in school, there is no calculus per se in high school. Therefore, some students study AP Calculus before going to college.

Using a Graphing Calculator

Graphical calculators are allowed on both the SAT and ACT tests, and the TI-83, TI-84, and the newer NSpire are the ones most commonly used in schools. Not all types of calculators (including those programmable) are allowed on the tests.

Many students use their calculators far too much. Many, for example, will not multiply 13 by 8 without a calculator! This is probably why the new SAT now contains one full section (with 20 problems) where the calculator is not allowed.

Most of the time you are not required to calculate the numerical value of π or radicals such as $\sqrt{2}$. For example, in multiple-choice questions, if the area of a circle is 25π, you may leave it as that and not calculate it to be 78.5. This helps save time.

In using the graphing facility, the student has to be fully familiar with the windows feature and adjust the scale as required by the problem. This sometimes involves trial and error and may take time.

The graphing aspect of a calculator certainly has its advantages. It is undoubtedly helpful in finding solutions to equations, both linear and quadratics. It may help you to understand a problem quickly and, for example, to immediately find the vertex, maxima, minima, etc.

Calculators are essential to evaluate permutations and combinations, matrices of the third and higher order, and much more. They are vital in the Math Subject Tests, Levels 1 and 2, where most of the answers are quantitative.

As a tutor, I hardly use a calculator in the regular tests. This is because, after years of practice, I am much more adept at mental arithmetic and in approximating results, which helps me quickly identify the multiple-choice answer closest my answer.

Equally important, I am often able to visualize linear, quadratic and other graphs without the use of the calculator and transform them quickly into a sketch. Graphing on the calculator takes time, and one can always introduce errors by incorrectly entering numbers, or the negative sign, or by forgetting brackets around fractions or exponents, etc.

Time Management

Mark and Move on!

When I first meet parents, they sometimes say to me that their child is a poor test-taker or that he or she has trouble with time management.

Not being able to complete a test on time means having dropped a few problems along the way or towards the end. This is almost the same as getting those problems wrong. I say "almost" because there is still negative marking in the math subject test, Levels 1&2.

These days, with no negative marking for incorrect answers in the main tests, you should try to guess the answers remaining. You have a 1-in-4 or 5 chance of getting the answer right with no penalty for being wrong!

To a large extent, time management can be taught to rectify the situation – but you must start by knowing how to solve problems. If you don't know the underlying math, you can spend a lot of time on a question and still not answer it correctly. So, do get to know your math and answer problems precisely.

If you know how to solve a problem, you will do so in a few seconds. If you don't know how to answer it, you may not be able to get the right answer in several minutes.

Please realize that with the SAT you have 25 minutes to do 20 problems in the first section, without a calculator. The second math section has 38 problems and allows 55 minutes, with a calculator. This broadly means an average of less than $1\frac{1}{2}$ minutes per question. Therefore, if you spend some 3 or 4 minutes on one problem, you are going to be short of time and run into trouble with the rest of the test. You will end up dropping several problems near the end of the test.

In order to avoid the foregoing situation, I suggest that you use a strategy described as "Mark and Move On". This essentially means that if you are not sure about a particular question, simply mark it and move on.

If you can answer the question, do so immediately. If you have no clue at all about a particular problem, just guess the answer promptly and move on. Don't waste any time.

In the in-between situation where you see a problem which you think you can solve if you attempt it, but are not entirely sure, don't tackle it immediately but mark it with your pencil and move on to the next problem. Do not spend any time on this question right now. If you decide to attempt it; spend 1 or 2 minutes on it; find that you cannot solve it, and then decide to mark it, please realize that you will have already lost that much time. If you don't spend any time on the question right now, you can always come back to it later if you have time at the end of the test. If you do not have any time left then, you have dropped a question you weren't sure about anyway.

To summarize, there are basically three types of math problems: Those which you can solve immediately; those you definitely cannot and those in-between. The first you should complete promptly. Those you don't know or understand, you can guess right away and forget about them. The third and last category is the hardest to deal with. If you are half sure about a particular problem, I suggest that you do not start it immediately. Mark it and move on! Your primary objective is to complete the entire test as quickly as possible. If you then have time left, you can come back and attempt the questions you marked earlier.

More Practical Tips

Sketching avoids errors

Practice, Practice, and Practice

While your child may be good at math in school and have also studied precalculus, it does not guarantee that he or she will do well on standardized tests. Why? The student has to be entirely familiar with the nature and style of SAT and ACT problems in order to complete them in the time available and score well.

I once had a student of Cuban origin who was doing advanced math with precalculus and had confidence in herself. When she took a sample test with her learning center, she did not even score 600. Perhaps the best thing that happened to her was that she came to the center where I was working. Now, I said, 'you will get ample practice with the tests and you should score over 700', and she did!

The best practical advice I can give anyone for the tests is to say: practice, practice, and practice with actual test problems. The more you do, the better you will be, without any doubt. If you walk into the test without any practice, you will not do as well, no matter how good or advanced you are in math. I have seen advanced students studying precalculus not score well in the SAT or ACT tests, mostly because they did not spend enough time on test problems.

There are any number of old test problems available publicly for practice. In addition to the College Board, which issues the tests, several publishers (Kaplan, Princeton, McGraw-Hill, Barron's, and others) sell books in shops or on Amazon, containing many tests with old SAT and ACT test problems. These books are not expensive and almost always contain answers with explanations. A relatively recent addition, Khan Academy, is available online.

I can vouch for the fact that the students who got perfect scores in the tests (800 in SAT and 36 in ACT) nearly always completed many problems and several books before actually taking their tests. It doesn't take all that long to complete one test, and it takes less and less time as you get better. Most students who practiced extensively rarely had trouble completing a math section or test within the time allowed and dropped fewer problems.

An additional tip: While practicing, it pays to keep track of the problems which you get wrong and which teach you something new. You should revise them later, immediately before the test. The family of a Japanese student who I taught for more than three years recorded all such problems and reviewed them 2 or 3 weeks before the test date. The student consistently scored 800 and planned on becoming an aeronautical engineer!

110-130 Different types of problems

There are probably some 110-130 different types of math problems included on the SAT or ACT. No one has ever counted them. It helps the test taker to be familiar with as many sorts of problems as possible in advance of the test. During the test, the student won't have time to experiment with answers or to learn new things. If they have seen a similar problem before and know how to solve it, it will take some 30 to 40 seconds to answer it. If not, it may take 3 to 4 minutes, and one cannot afford the extra time.

Read carefully, and again

If you cannot figure out a problem, try reading it again and again, if time allows. It helps to break the problem down bit by bit and see if it then makes sense. If the problem is still not clear, try plugging in any number or, maybe, use one of the multiple-choice answers, and it might come to life. Or sketch something. It does not take long and may help you visualize things better.

Shortcuts

In the SAT and ACT tests there are often built-in shortcuts, and it is important to look for them. You may not see them unless you look for them consciously. This happens especially with simultaneous equations in two variables x and y. Sometimes you can solve the equations simply by adding or subtracting them instead of going the long, conventional way of solving by elimination or substitution. For example:

$2x - 3y = 4$

$3x - 2y = 5$

If you are asked for the value of (x+y), go looking for it directly by subtracting the first equation from the second. You will find that $x+y=1$. (Finding $x=\dfrac{7}{5}$ and $y=\dfrac{-2}{5}$ separately would take too long!)

A general rule should be to always simplify numbers, fractions, expressions, and equations as much as possible before attempting to find shortcuts. This should be an almost automatic process and, if this is not done, the student may not see the shortcut.

They are not out to trick you

Let me say that, while I have seen the odd or weird problem in my time, the College Board, who designs the tests, is not there to trick students or trap them into wrong answers. Their objective is to have the same level of testing for all students nationwide and to fairly assess an individual student's knowledge and skills in math relative to others. It is not easy to compare teaching standards in remote areas in, say, Alabama, with top schools in New York City.

Mark answer sheets correctly

Understand how to write your answers on the computer sheets and place them correctly. If the student misaligns one answer, several subsequent answers could be wrong, leading to a series of errors.

At the test center

The student should go to sleep early the night before the test. He or she must take a calculator and a watch to the test center. Arrive a few minutes early at the center since being even a few minutes late may disorient the person. And, good luck!

Get a hard copy of this book

Kindle does an excellent job of presenting this book to the reader on various electronic devices, including the cell phone. However, since this is a book for constant study, it may make more sense to get a hard copy so that you can easily make notes, highlight sections, and write points to remember.

Top test takers are those who aim to get 800 on their SAT or 36 on the ACT, or as close as possible. There are surprisingly more of them than you may imagine!

These students need to make a conscious effort to get each and every problem right. This requires focus, concentration, lots of practice with all types of possible problems, and increased fluency in solving them. Accuracy, accuracy, and accuracy is the watchword.

One error and the student would have blown a perfect score!

Extensive practice with varied problems is an essential ingredient. Next, read carefully, extra carefully. One word omitted or read wrong can change the answer. Words like integer, odd, even, positive, negative, inclusive, additional, another, etc. are vitally important.

On one memorable occasion, when privately tutoring a Russian student for the regular SAT, I spent two hours trying to see if he would make one mistake! I failed. At the end of the session, in amazement, I asked him what he planned to score in the test the following Saturday. 800 he said and, a few weeks later, confirmed it. He was the son of a nuclear physicist!

Sometimes, no matter how well you prepare, you may come across a problem you have never seen before and cannot make any sense of it. This would be, what I call, an odd-ball problem and all the student can do is rise to the occasion and do the best they can. Other students will also face the same problem.

Overachievers often do the Math Subject Tests before taking the regular SAT. The Subject Tests in Math, Levels 1 & 2, not only involve a higher level of math but also have a different style. Therefore, they increase the student's level of competence and confidence in math.

Both the Level 1 & Level 2 Math Subject Tests are 1-hour tests with 50 problems each. Level 2 has a generous grading curve, and it is not all that hard to score 800 – even with 3 or 4 wrong answers! – if you know the math.

On passing the math subject tests, acceptance to colleges becomes easier, and scholarships more attainable. Plus, the extra knowledge of math will undoubtedly help the student in college with all subjects.

The weaker student

It may sound paradoxical, but after studying this book, it should be easier for a student who is weaker at math to improve their score more than a top student. This is because the former starts from a lower level and can quickly pick up several ideas from this book. The stronger student already knows more and obviously has less room to move up in scores. (I wish all students success in the tests and would love to hear from them eventually.)

A few students may have some kind of learning disability and need more support. They require more tutoring with constant repetition. Good students grasp the logic of an argument quickly, but the weaker students either do not appreciate the logic or are unable to remember what they have learned.

In both standardized tests, the student may apply for special accommodations to counteract certain disabilities. Parents should speak to guidance counselors at school and follow their advice.

From experience, I have found that if the weaker student is given 50% or 100% extra time in tests, they are more or less compensated and will score well. There are other less significant accommodations available, and you can obtain specific advice from the counselor.

Weaker students should pay particular attention to my advice on Time Management, provided earlier in an independent section in this book. A high achiever rarely has trouble completing all math problems in the time allowed. This is often not the case with less-gifted students; they frequently run out of time and are not able to complete the tests.

It is imperative for these students to use the Mark and Move On strategy: Answer the problems you can do immediately; promptly guess the questions you have no clue about and mark the in-betweens to come back to later, if you have the time. Do not spend an inordinate amount of time on any one problem.

On Scoring the Test

A scoring table tells you exactly how much you scored, depending on how many problems you get right, wrong, or omit. Each test has its own scoring table, and these vary slightly between tests. You can locate a sample scoring table by using Google. Make sure you have a table for the new SAT (with 20 and 38 problems in the two sections).

The student most likely has some idea of what he or she would like to score on the math test. The scoring table tells you exactly how many problems you can get wrong and still achieve the target score. For example, if your goal is 600, you will see that you can afford to get as many as 23 problems out of the total 58 problems wrong on the SAT test. Similarly, to get 27 on the ACT, you can get some 25 out of 60 problems wrong. Thus, you will see that there is ample room for errors, and this should help you sleep easier at night!

While I am on the subject of scoring, I would like to mention that you should take extra care to mark the computer answer sheets correctly. If you misalign one answer by placing it in the wrong box, your subsequent answers are also likely to be placed incorrectly, and you will have a string of errors, devastating your overall score.

In order to improve the score, you should practice continuously with actual SAT and ACT tests and keep track of how many problems you get wrong each time. Focus on reducing this number until you reach your target scores or better. Practice makes perfect!

A Word to Parents

When I first meet parents, they sometimes tell me that their child does well in math in school, scoring maybe 90-95% on recent tests. This usually does not impress me until I know which school they attend. More importantly, I need to know what level of math class the student is in – regular, advanced or honors. (Not all schools have the same tier system.) Students in honors classes do very well in standardized math tests since the level of math taught to them is higher. Students in the regular math class are taught basic math and it is not easy for them to achieve similar good scores in the SAT or ACT tests. My constant advice to parents is to recognize this tier system and strive to have their child placed in the highest math level possible in school. The school, on their part, will not accept a student unless they have some confidence that the student can cope with that particular level of math.

The national average SAT math score is around 520, given that the score ranges from about 240 to the maximum score of 800. In my view, a student with a score of less than 520 is weak in math; a score between 520 and 650 is average (particularly in my counties of Westchester, NY and Fairfield, CT). My dividing line on whether or not a student is good in math is 650 – above this level he or she is good at math, and over 700 is close to excellent. As for the ACT, the maximum score is 36 and the minimum is 1, with a national average score of around 21.

Now, a word about tutors: Parents often assume that all it takes to be a good math teacher is an excellent knowledge of the math subjects. This is a short-sighted view and, in my opinion, a tutor must also know how to communicate with a student and, equally importantly, be able to motivate him or her to perform better. My own motto in teaching is Communication, Motivation & Excellence (CME).

If you do not have access to an experienced math tutor with a track record, your best bet may be to contact one of the many large learning centers around, such as Kaplan, Princeton, Huntington, etc. However, do remember that they charge a fair amount of money, while many of their tutors are part-timers or inexperienced.

Tutors.com, Skype or math tutorial courses on the Internet generally do not provide the level of proficiency necessary for a student to get into a college or university of his or her choice, or attract attractive scholarships. Only dedicated self-study and individual tutoring with an experienced teacher can increase a student's knowledge of math sufficiently.

Whether the student decides to choose SAT or ACT (or, in fact, both), and if the student is reasonably competent in math, I suggest that he or she also consider taking the Subject Tests in SAT Math, Levels 1 & 2. Some students take these subject tests before their regular SAT or ACT Tests. This is helpful to them and expands their knowledge of and confidence in math. (Level 2 is a continuation of the level of difficulty of Level 1 and, being scored liberally, enables higher math scores.)

Scholarships granted are not necessarily dependent on high scores achieved. There are many criteria for colleges to determine scholarships, including sports and extracurricular activities. Sometimes, these scholarships cover four full years of college. Other colleges may provide special awards to students who show the most improvement in scores over time.

The students who do the best on standardized tests are those who spend a lot of time on their own practicing math problems. It is important to think on one's own. For this reason, when I am their tutor, I insist on the student doing some homework in between sessions. The homework is not intended to be a burden but merely keep the student thinking about the subject matter of study.

Finally, if a child has learning or attention issues, it makes sense to apply for special accommodations for both the SAT and ACT tests. This could be in the form of an extra 50% or 100% time for the tests or other facilities. These help improve the student's test scores significantly.

Accommodations are different for SAT and ACT, and parents have to apply to the College Board for the SAT or the ACT organization. Necessary documentation to establish the need for accommodations must be provided, and the process of getting approval may take two or more months. It is better to apply through the student's school since they know the process better. Standard request forms are available on websites and must be used, and the school may also have to countersign. Accommodations are possible for SAT, ACT, PSAT and AP Tests.

For Students

This book reads very well on most smartphones and is particularly useful for teenagers, who are nearly always on their cell phones. Using the hyperlinks embedded in the table of contents, they can use their phones at their convenience to focus on the subjects of most interest to them as well as move freely from one topic to another.

Teenagers have short attention spans, whereas most of the math books written on the SAT and ACT Tests run up to several hundreds of pages. My deliberate aim, therefore, has been to keep this book as short as possible while covering all the relevant math topics. I would like you to read all of this book and get a full view of the landscape. This is likely to get you more interested in the subject matter, become motivated, work harder, and perform well on the tests. There will be parts of the book which you will not understand immediately, but that does not matter so much presently. The important point is to be patient and continue with the process, and it will inevitably benefit you.

While I appear to have achieved my basic objectives above, I have received a few comments that this book does not contain enough explanations or illustrations for some of the mathematical concepts described in the book. I have therefore compiled a set of a few additional, standard-sized pages of examples of the techniques explained in this book, cross-referenced to the chapter titles or slogans in the book. I will happily send it in pdf format, free of cost or obligation to anyone who contacts me at the email address alpashamg@gmail.com.

As I have explained in this book, to do well on the tests, you have first to understand the nature and structure of the tests. Thereafter, practice, practice, and more practice is essential. There are dozens of books written on these tests from reputable publishers available on Amazon or in the bookshops. They give many test problems with full explanations and are not expensive. Get two or three of these books and practice. As you get better, skip the easier problems and focus on the harder ones. These difficult problems have been described fully in this book and, for example, on the ACT, they constitute the last ten problems.

Once you have read the book or sooner, I would request you to write a brief review of the book based on your experience. Your good reviews will help me reach and benefit many more students, whereas the critical ones would help improve the book. Writing a review on Amazon is easy enough to do and should not take more than 3 to 5 minutes of your time. You would need to write a minimum of 20 words, which really means two or three sentences only.

Find this book's exclusive page on Amazon's website by typing MATH GOLD and go all the way down on the left-hand side to get to the customer reviews section. I will thank you now in anticipation for your time and for what you write there.

Finally, let me wish you tremendous success on your SAT, ACT and Math Subject Tests. I certainly hope that you find remarkable success (or math gold!) in terms of improvement in your scores on the tests. Let me know!

AL PASHA

Al Pasha was born in India, lived in Europe, and has been an American citizen for many years. He lives in Connecticut and spends much of his time in New York.

Having studied math professionally, he taught math full-time in the Sacred Heart Academy, followed by ten years as an Elite Math Tutor with the Kaplan Learning Center. Since then, and for the last seven years, he has been an independent private math tutor in the Fairfield and Westchester counties. During this period, he has taught over 700 students in regular math, SAT, ACT, SAT II (Levels 1&2), and AP Calculus, producing excellent results.

He was married and has a son and a daughter. The latter scored 800 in SAT Math, attended an Ivy League University, and became a senior corporate executive at the age of 35.

His website www.calculus-math-tutor.com provides more details about his teaching skills and experience, with many testimonials.

The website for his books is www.mathgold.net. He can be reached at alpashaipi@aol.com.

Books by Al Pasha

SAT/ACT Math Gold

How to dramatically improve your high school math score in three or four weeks without a private tutor.

SAT/ACT Math Gold tpe
Teachers & Parents Edition

How teachers and parents can help their students and kids improve their math scores in high school and on the SAT/ACT tests.

Keep Math Simple!
How to be a better Math tutor

How teachers and parents can help their students improve their math scores in high school and on standardized tests.

www.mathgold.net

alpashamg@gmail.com

All three books are available on
www.Amazon.com.
The first few pages of these books can be viewed there for free.

Made in the USA
Coppell, TX
17 April 2020